HORSE RIDER'S YEARBOOK

David & Charles

A DAVID & CHARLES BOOK

First published in the UK in 2003

Copyright © David & Charles 2003

Distributed in North America
by F&W Publications, Inc.
4700 East Galbraith Road
Cincinnati, OH 45236
1-800-289-0963

Every effort has been made to locate all persons having rights to the extracts
appearing in this book, and to secure permission from the holders of such rights.

Extract from *Riding: The True Techniques* reprinted by permission of PFD on behalf of
Lucy Rees.
Extract from *Dancing with Horses* by Klaus Ferdinand Hempfling reprinted by permis-
sion of J.A. Allen (first published in Britain in 2001).
Blessings by Edric Roberts reproduced by kind permission of *The Field* magazine.

A catalogue record for this book is available from the British Library.

ISBN 0 7153 1659 1

Printed in Singapore by KHL Printing Co Pte Ltd
for David & Charles
Brunel House   Newton Abbot   Devon

Commissioning Editor: Jane Trollope
Designer: Lisa Forrester
Desk Editor: Shona Wallis
Text supplied and edited by Jo Weeks
Production Controller: Ros Napper

Visit our website at www.davidandcharles.co.uk

David & Charles books are available from all good bookshops; alternatively you can
contact our Orderline on (0)1626 334555 or write to us at FREEPOST EX2110,
David & Charles Direct, Newton Abbot, TQ12 4ZZ (no stamp required UK mainland).

CONTENTS

About me

Name *Andrea Cannon*

Address *2 New Field Drive North Tyne Lincoln*

Phone home/work *01526 860573   860630*

Mobile *0771 5550219*

Email *Alialoaf 02 .co.uk*

Driving licence number/car registration *VLoiGna*

Trailer/lorry serial numbers

Passport number/renewal date

National insurance number *JP17673*

Blood group

Breakdown assistance membership

Hat size *55*

Glove size *Small*

Shoe size/calf height and width *S*

Jacket size

Jodphur size/leg length

Body protector size

Useful phone numbers

Livery yard

Vet

Farrier

Equine dentist

Doctor

Dentist

Complementary therapist

Equine insurer

Local police station

Feed merchant

Forage merchant

Bedding merchant

Riding school/instructor

Rug cleaner/repairer

Saddler/tack shop H cRobinson

Tack repairer

Builder/carpenter

Bridleways officer/park ranger(s)

Equine charity(ies)

Car insurer (and policy number)

Property insurer (and policy number)

Others

Your vet

- Get to know your vet before you need him or her in an emergency. Even with a very healthy horse, your vet will need to visit once a year to give vaccinations. You should get on well and be able to discuss any concerns about your horse's health. If you feel you aren't on the same wavelength, consider changing vets – sooner rather than later.

- If you keep your horse at a livery yard, make sure the owner has your vet's name and contact number and is aware of any important information about your horse's health.

Your equine dentist

- Your vet may be able to look after your horse's teeth, otherwise ask him or her to recommend a good dentist.

- See p.20 for information about dental treatment.

Electrical safety

When using electrical equipment, such as clippers, near horses always practise extreme care:

✔ Check the equipment, particularly the flex, and use a circuit breaker plug – every single time you use it.

✔ Ensure the flex is well out of the way of the horse's hooves and teeth.

✔ Ensure you, your hands, the horse and the area you are in are all dry.

✔ If you suspect electrocution, switch off the electric supply or use dry wood, such as a broom handle, to remove the electric equipment from the person (see also 'First aid for people', p.26).

What is microchipping?

Microchipping involves inserting a small microchip under the skin of your horse's neck. It causes no discomfort to him and means he is easily reunited with you should he go missing or be stolen.

About COCO

Age 15 coco 12 Bradley

Height 14·2hh 15hh

Sex mare gelding

Breed Hackney Connemara

Colour Liverchestnut dark grey

Face markings Start +snip Blaze

Leg and feet markings 2 White socks N/A

Other distinctive marks little whiteads

Saddle size and length, make, serial number
16½ wintee wide 17" Ideal wide

Bridle size COB COB

Rug size 5'9 6'0

Passport life number

Heart rate

Temperature

Respiration rate

Weight

Freeze mark

Microchip

Insurance policy number

Date of purchase

History

Previous owner and how long they owned him/her

Sire/dam

Breed registration certificate number

Body protectors

Buying a body protector

- Measurements you will need: waist, chest, waist-to-waist – from waist at the back, over your shoulder to waist at the front.
- Choose the correct size using the charts supplied with all BETA (British Equine Trade Association) standard protectors.
- Try on the protector over light clothing – heavier clothing is best over the top.
- Adjust to fit closely, using the straps and fastenings.
- Wear it for about 5 minutes in the shop to ensure it is still comfortable when it has moulded to your body shape.

Does it fit?

- ✔ It reaches your breastbone at the front and the base of your neck at the back.
- ✔ It fits around your body.
- ✔ It finishes just below your ribs (2.5cm/1in) at the front.
- ✔ It covers your collar bones.
- ✔ It wouldn't push up at the back (too long) when you sit in the saddle.
- ✔ It is comfortable in all riding positions – try these out as far as possible in the shop before you buy.

BETA 2000 Standard in brief

Level 1 (black label)
Low level of protection for licensed jockeys only.

Level 2 (brown label)
For use in low-risk situations only. NOT for jumping, riding on roads, riding young horses, riding excitable horses. NOT for inexperienced riders.

Level 3 (purple label)
Appropriate for normal horse riding and competitions.

Riding hats

To find your size measure the circumference of your head, just above your ears, preferably using a tape marked with centimetres. Choose hats that meet at least one of the following safety standards – BSEN1384 (British Standards Institute) or PAS015 or ASTM F1163/SEI (American Society for Testing and Materials/Safety Equipment Institute). New hats have an easy-to-understand star rating to ensure you pick the most suitable for you.

Size guide

Head size (cm)	Riding hat	Jockey skull
51	6¼	00
52	6⅜	00½
53	6½	0
54	6⅝	0½
55	6¾	1
56	6⅞	1½
57	7	2
58	7⅛	2½
59	7¼	3
60	7¼	3½
61	7½	4
62	7⅝	4½
63	7¾	5

What size rug or blanket?

Get a tape measure and place one end in the middle of your horse's chest. Get someone to take the other end around his side, holding it at the same level, to the middle of his back legs, below the top of the tail. Rug sizes are in increments of 3 inches – for example 51in, 54in, 57in. If your horse falls between increments, a rug that is slightly too large is usually better than one that is slightly too small. Some rugs are fuller than others, or more adjustable. Look carefully before you buy as few places will exchange rugs.

About _Bradley_

Age _13_

Height _14.2hh_

Sex _Gelding_

Breed _Connemara_

Colour _Grey_

Face markings _Blaze_

Leg and feet markings

Other distinctive marks

Saddle size and length, make, serial number

Bridle size

Rug size

Passport life number

Heart rate

Temperature

Respiration rate

Weight

Freeze mark

Microchip

Insurance policy number

Date of purchase

History

Previous owner and how long they owned him/her

Sire/dam

Breed registration certificate number

Shoe sizes

Children

UK	6	7	8	9	9½	10	11	12	12½	13	1	2	2½	3
Continental	23	24	25	26	27	28	29	30	31	32	33	34	35	36

Adult

UK	4	5	6	6½	7	8	9	9½	10	11	12
Continental	37	38	39	40	41	42	43	44	45	46	47

Clothes sizes

Men

UK	36	38	40	42	44	46
US	36	38	40	42	44	46
Continental	46	48	50	52	54	56

Women

UK	10	12	14	16	18	20
US	8	10	12	14	16	18
Continental	38	40	42	44	46	48

Children (these sizes are very approximate)

US	3	4	6	8	10
Height (cm)	100	110	120	130	155
Age	3–4	4–5	6–8	8–10	10–12

Linear conversions

To convert

inches to centimetres multiply by 2.54cm

centimetres to inches multiply by 0.3937

feet to metres multiply by 0.3048

metres to feet multiply by 3.2808

In these quick-reference conversions the figures have been rounded up or down.

ft/in	m/cm		cm	in		m	ft		hh	cm
1in	2.5cm		1cm	½in		1m	3¼ft		10	102
2in	5cm		2cm	¾in		2m	6½ft		10.2	107
3in	7.5cm		3cm	1¼in		3m	10ft		11	112
4in	10cm		4cm	1½in		4m	13ft		11.2	117
5in	12.5cm		5cm	2in		5m	16½ft		12	122
6in	15cm		6cm	2½in		6m	19½ft		12.2	127
1ft	30cm		7cm	2¾in		7m	23ft		13	132
1ft 6in	45cm		8cm	3in		8m	26¼ft		13.2	137
2ft	60cm		9cm	3½in		9m	29½ft		14	142
2ft 6in	75cm		10cm	4in		10m	33ft		14.2	148
3ft	90cm		11cm	4¼in		11m	36ft		15	153
3ft 6in	1.06m		12cm	4¾in		12m	39½ft		15.2	158
4ft	1.20m		13cm	5in		13m	42½ft		16	163
4ft 6in	1.40m		14cm	5½in		14m	46ft			
5ft	1.50m		15cm	6in		15m	49¼ft			
5ft 6in	1.65m		20cm	8in		20m	65½ft			
6ft	1.80m									

About

Age

Height

Sex

Breed

Colour

Face markings

Leg and feet markings

Other distinctive marks

Saddle size and length, make, serial number

Bridle size

Rug size

Passport life number

Heart rate

Temperature

Respiration rate

Weight

Freeze mark

Microchip

Insurance policy number

Date of purchase

History

Previous owner and how long they owned him/her

Sire/dam

Breed registration certificate number

Weight conversions

To convert

ounces to grams	multiply by 28.3494
grams to ounces	multiply by 0.0353
pounds to kilograms	multiply by 0.4536
kilograms to pounds	multiply by 2.2046

In these quick-reference conversions the figures have been rounded up or down.

ounces	grams
1oz	28g
2oz	56g
3oz	85g
4oz	113g
5oz	142g

grams	ounces
15g	½oz
20g	¾oz
30g	1oz
35g	1¼oz
40g	1½oz
45g	1½oz
50g	1¾oz

pounds	kilograms
1lb	0.45kg
2lb	0.90kg
3lb	1.4kg
4lb	1.8kg
5lb	2.25kg

kilograms	pounds
1kg	2lb4oz
2kg	4lb7oz
3kg	6lb10oz
4kg	8lb13oz
5kg	11lb

Liquid conversions

To convert

fluid ounces to millilitres	multiply by 28.4
millilitres to fluid ounces	multiply by 0.3519
pints to litres	multiply by 0.5682
litres to pints	multiply by 1.7598

In these quick-reference conversions the figures have been rounded up or down.

fluid ounces	litres
2fl/oz	57ml
4fl/oz	114ml
6fl/oz	170ml
8fl/oz	227ml
10fl/oz	280ml
20fl/oz	560ml

millilitres	fluid ounces
10ml	3½fl/oz
20ml	7fl/oz
30ml	10½fl/oz
40ml	14fl/oz
50ml	17½fl/oz

pints	litres
1pt	0.5l
2pt	1l
3pt	1.5l
4pt	2.25l
5pt	3l
10pt	5.5l

litres	pints
1l	2pt
2l	3½pt
3l	5pt
4l	7pt
5l	8¾pt

January	February	March
1T	1S	1M
2F	2M	2T
3S	3T	3W
4S	4W	4T
5M	5T	5F
6T	6F	6S
7W	7S	7S
8T	8S	8M
9F	9M	9T
10S	10T	10W
11S	11W	11T
12M	12T	12F
13T	13F	13S
14W	14S	14S
15T	15S	15M
16F	16M	16T
17S	17T	17W
18S	18W	18T
19M	19T	19F
20T	20F	20S
21W	21S	21S
22T	22S	22M
23F	23M	23T
24S	24T	24W
25S	25W	25T
26M	26T	26F
27T	27F	27S
28W	28S	28S
29T	29S	29M
30F		30T
31S		31W

Getting organized

Don't forget to include:

Shoeing – every 4–6 weeks, possibly more often in summer

Vet's visits for routine vaccinations – once a year for equine flu and tetanus

Dentist's visit – every 6 months

Saddler's visit – every 6 months/annually

Worming – at least 5 times a year (see 'A worming calendar', opposite)

Horse shows – fitness schedules and a preparation countdown

Your holiday – remember to organize some-one to care for your horse well in advance

April

1T
2F
3S
4S
5M
6T
7W
8T
9F
10S
11S
12M
13T
14W
15T
16F
17S
18S
19M
20T
21W
22T
23F
24S
25S
26M
27T
28W
29T
30F

May

1S
2S
3M
4T
5W
6T
7F
8S
9S
10M
11T
12W
13T
14F
15S
16S
17M
18T
19W
20T
21F
22S
23S
24M
25T
26W
27T
28F
29S
30S
31M

June

1T
2W
3T
4F
5S
6S
7M
8T
9W
10T
11F
12S
13S
14M
15T
16W
17T
18F
19S
20S
21M
22T
23W
24T
25F
26S
27S
28M
29T
30W

A worming calendar

When?	What for?	What with?
Sep–Oct	tapeworm	pyrantel or praziquantel (eg Strongid-P, Equimax)
Nov–Dec	encysted small redworm, large redworm (larvae and adults), seat worm	fenbendazole (eg Panacur Equine Guard)
Nov–Dec, after frosts	bots	ivermectin (eg Eqvalan)
Feb	as Dec for vulnerable horses (*)	fenbendazole (eg Panacur Equine Guard)
Mar to Sep, every 4–13 weeks (**)	routine, grazing-season worming (***)	

(*)Youngsters or those on heavily grazed pasture. (**)Administer every 4–13 weeks, depending on wormer used. (***)Make a note of the wormer you use this year and change to another one for the grazing season next year. Rotate annually, not at each dose, so for example, in year 1 use ivermectin, year 2 fenbendazole, year 3 praziquantel with ivermectin, year 4 pyrantel, year 5 moxidectin.

July
1T
2F
3S
4S
5M
6T
7W
8T
9F
10S
11S
12M
13T
14W
15T
16F
17S
18S
19M
20T
21W
22T
23F
24S
25S
26M
27T
28W
29T
30F
31S

August
1S
2M
3T
4W
5T
6F
7S
8S
9M
10T
11W
12T
13F
14S
15S
16M
17T
18W
19T
20F
21S
22S
23M
24T
25W
26T
27F
28S
29S
30M
31T

September
1W
2T
3F
4S
5S
6M
7T
8W
9T
10F
11S
12S
13M
14T
15W
16T
17F
18S
19S
20M
21T
22W
23T
24F
25S
26S
27M
28T
29W
30T

Worming record
Record the date and brand/type you use.

1...
2...
3...
4...
5...
6...
7...
8...

About wormers

✔ Good hygiene, particularly removing manure from paddocks, is crucial to worm control (see p.38).

✔ Before worming, weigh your horse (p.34) to ensure you give the correct dose.

✔ Consider getting an annual worm count done on a manure sample to check your worming regime is working.

October

1F
2S
3S
4M
5T
6W
7T
8F
9S
10S
11M
12T
13W
14T
15F
16S
17S
18M
19T
20W
21T
22F
23S
24S
25M
26T
27W
28T
29F
30S
31S

November

1M
2T
3W
4T
5F
6S
7S
8M
9T
10W
11T
12F
13S
14S
15M
16T
17W
18T
19F
20S
21S
22M
23T
24W
25T
26F
27S
28S
29M
30T

December

1W
2T
3F
4S
5S
6M
7T
8W
9T
10F
11S
12S
13M
14T
15W
16T
17F
18S
19S
20M
21T
22W
23T
24F
25S
26S
27M
28T
29W
30T
31F

Below are the main drugs used in wormers; read the label to find out what your wormer contains

- Fenbendazol (Benzimidazole Group) kills large and small redworm, and the 5-day treatment will kill encysted small redworm. Doesn't kill tapeworm or bots, not hugely effective against lungworm. Lasts for 6 weeks.

- Praziquantel (Macrocyclic Lactone Group) kills tapeworm and all other worms when combined with ivermectin, as in the wormer Equimax, which lasts 8–10 weeks.

- Ivermectin (Macrocyclic Lactone Group) kills all worms except tapeworm. Lasts for 8 weeks.

- Moxidectin (Macrocyclic Lactone Group) kills all worms except tapeworm. May kill some encysted small redworm. Lasts for 13 weeks.

- Pyrantel (Pyrimidine Group) kills tapeworm when double dosed. Doesn't kill bots, lungworm, encysted small redworm. Lasts for 6 weeks.

A record of my costs

Keeping a record of all your costs and how they arose will enable you to improve your budgeting skills for next year as well as build up a history of your horse for future reference. It might also show you where you could cut down or improve efficiency.

	Date	Details	Cost
Feed/forage			
			total

	Date	Details	Cost
Bedding			
			total

	Date	Details	Cost
Livery			
			total

	Date	Details	Cost
Dentist			
			total

	Date	Details	Cost
Vet			
		total	

Farrier			
		total	

Other specialists			
		total	

Other expenditure

Include here all other items: insurance, riding lessons, wormers, rugs, saddle and rug repairs, new grooming kit, riding clothes, horsey treats, riding club and magazine subscriptions, entry and transport to competitions, clipping fees.

		total	

| grand total | | | |

Points of the horse

forehead
eye
cheek
nostril
lips
ear
chin groove
poll
throat
crest
jugular groove
neck
shoulder
point of shoulder
mane
breast
wither
elbow
forearm
knee
cannon
fetlock
pastern
hoof
back
loins
chest
girth
point of elbow
chestnut
flexor tendons
ergot
coronary band
heel
croup
flank
stifle
cannon
fetlock
pastern
hoof
point of hip
abdomen
dock
point of buttock
thigh
tail
gaskin (second thigh)
point of hock
hock joint
ergot
coronary band
heel

Skeleton

ischium (point of buttock)

axis
atlas
temporo-
mandibular joint

cervical vertebrae (7)

orbit of eye

sacrum (5
fused vertebrae)

lumbar vertebrae (6)

thoracic vertebrae (18)

caudal vertebrae
(16)

nasal bone

hip joint

mandible
(lower jaw)
maxilla
(upper jaw)

femur

scapula (shoulder bone)

shoulder joint

pelvis

humerus

ribs (36)

elbow joint

stifle joint

sternum

radius

fibula

olecranon
(point of elbow)
ulna

tibia

carpus (knee joint)

calcaneus
(point of hock)

tarsus
(hock joint)

cannon (3rd metatarsal)

splint

fetlock joint

long pastern (2nd metatarsal)

short pastern (1st metatarsal)

sesamoid

pedal (coffin) bone

navicular

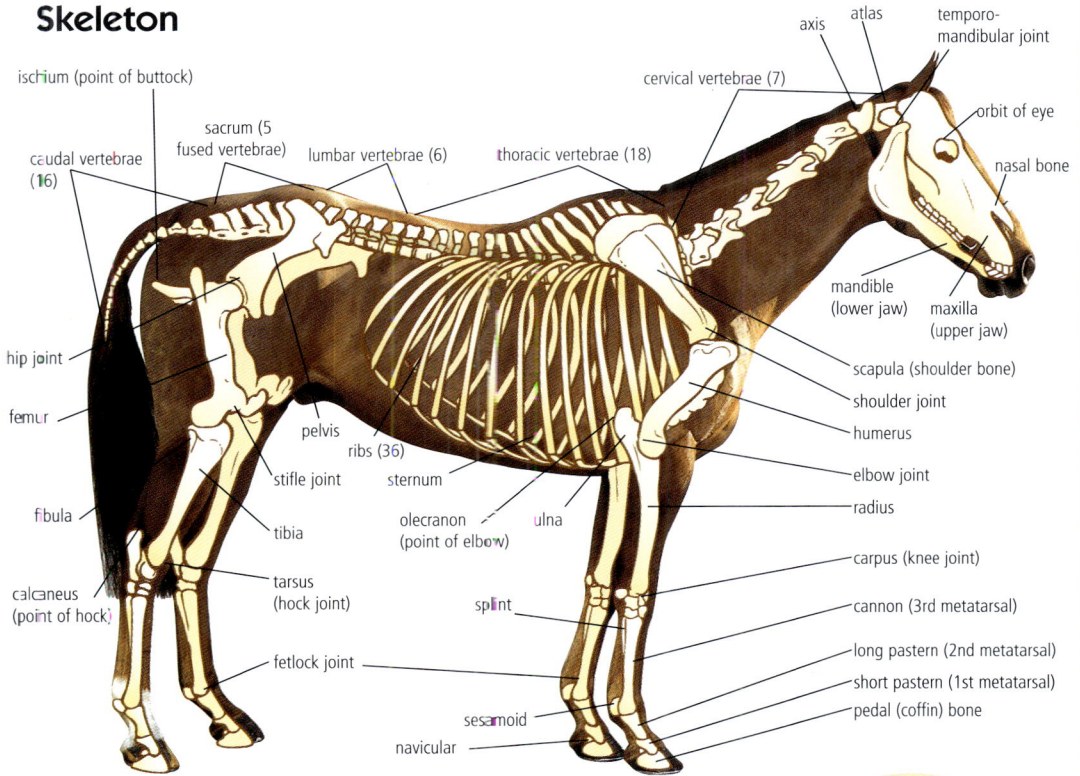

Some definitions

- **Arteries** carry blood away from the heart. A cut artery pulses as it bleeds.

- **Bones** are a store for minerals and the marrow, which produces red blood cells.

- **Bursae** are sacs found near joints, such as the knee, or bony areas, such as the poll. They contain the lubricating synovial fluid

- **Cartilage** is a smooth tough substance that allows smooth movement of the joints.

- **Collagen** is a fibrous tissue found in bones and tendons.

- **Joints** are found where ever two bones meet. Their ends are covered with cartilage and the most flexible joints, such as knees, hocks and fetlocks, are lubricated by synovial fluid produced by synovial membranes in the bursae.

- **Ligaments** attach bones to bones and consist of fibrous tissue in rigid bands.

- **Muscles** are made of fibrous tissue. They are usually connected to bones via tendons.

- **Tendons** attach muscles to bones and consist of collagen. They are not as flexible as muscles, which is why tendons are more usually strained than muscles. Flexor tendons flex the muscles, while extensor tendons extend them – so a leg is lifted by a flexor tendon and moved forward by an extensor tendon.

- **Veins** carry blood to the heart. A cut vein bleeds as a steady flow.

A horse's body:

✦ is 65% water
✦ contains up to 45 litres (79 pints) of blood
✦ produces up to 20kg (44lbs) of faeces and 9 litres (16 pints) of urine daily

Teeth and dental health

Some definitions

- **Adult teeth** These are large and yellow. It takes about six months from when they appear to when they are large enough to come into use.
- **Cup** The hole in the table (grinding surface), which gradually gets shallower as the teeth wear away with age. In the young horse its appearance is long and narrow on the table, with age it becomes oval and then triangular.
- **Dental star** A raised, brown-stained area on the table that consists of additional dentine, which grows to protect the nerves as the teeth are worn down.
- **Dentine** The hard substance that the teeth are mostly made from.
- **Galvayne's groove** A dark-coloured groove that begins to grow down the upper corner incisors at 9 or 10 years old.
- **Incisors** The row of teeth at the front of the mouth on both jaws.
- **Mark** When it has become very shallow, the cup is called the mark.
- **Milk teeth** These are baby teeth. They are small and white and are pointed where they emerge from the gum.
- **Molars** The large teeth at the back of the jaw, sometimes called cheek teeth.
- **Table** The grinding surface of the tooth.
- **Temporomandibular joint** The joint that joins the upper and lower jaws (see p.19). Poorly cared for teeth can inhibit the movement of this joint, which in turn may cause pain and hence behavioural problems.
- **Tushes** Small canine teeth mostly found in male horses, these grow near the corner incisors on both jaws and sometimes cause bitting problems.
- **Wolf teeth** Tiny teeth just in front of the first molars on both jaws. These often cause discomfort and are nearly always removed.

When to call the dentist

A dentist should visit your horse every six months. As well as these regular check ups, consider calling the dentist if your horse:

- starts being difficult to ride, or performs less well than usual;
- throws his head around or rears;
- develops a dislike of the bit or having the noseband done up;
- keeps putting his tongue over the bit;
- keeps putting his tongue out of his mouth when wearing a bridle;
- has any difficulty eating, including dropping food (quidding), bolting food, eating hay in preference to hard food, choking.

Common dental problems

- **Teething** – up to the age of 5 new teeth may cause discomfort and milk teeth may need to be removed when they are ready to be replaced by adult teeth.
- **Wolf teeth** – these need removal if they are uncomfortable or in the way of the bit.
- **Sharp edges** – the teeth grow continuously and are ground down by the horse eating. Uneven wear can produce sharp edges on the molars – on the outer edge of the upper jaw molars and the inner edge of the lower jaw molars.

Indicators of a painful mouth

✦ Discharge from eyes or nostrils
✦ Sensitive cheeks or lumps on jaw
✦ Excessive drooling
✦ Irregular movement of lower jaw
✦ Inability to shift lower jaw from side to side
✦ Bad breath
✦ Sores or bleeding on the lips, gums, palate
✦ Longer than normal particles in the manure
✦ Weight loss or poor condition despite good feeding

Dental treatment

Usual treatment consists of the dentist using a selection of rasps to smooth off all the sharp edges on the teeth, including the molars at the back of the mouth – this is called floating. Plaque may also be removed from the tushes. A gag holds the horse's mouth open and he is held steady with a headcollar. The dentist will need a bucket of clean water and a clean well-lit stable or enclosed area. For removal of wolf teeth and more difficult or painful dentistry, such as dealing with abcesses, an anaesthetic may be used.

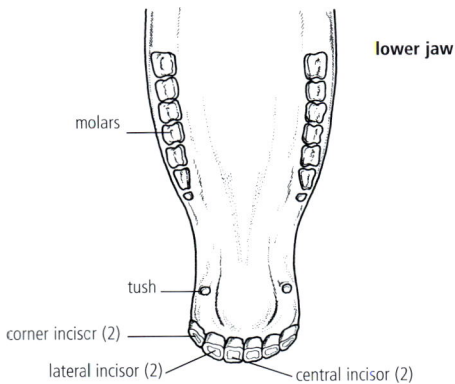

lower jaw

molars

tush

corner incisor (2)

lateral incisor (2)

central incisor (2)

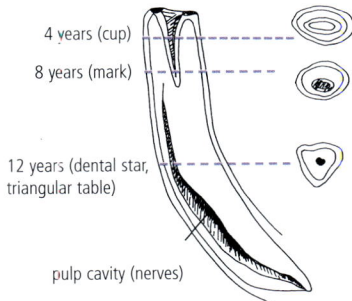

cross section through incisor   table (grinding surface)

4 years (cup)

8 years (mark)

12 years (dental star, triangular table)

pulp cavity (nerves)

Ageing

A horse's age can be estimated by its incisors, particularly when young. With age the table alters from oval to triangular, the deep cup wears away, until it becomes the shallow 'mark', the dental star appears on the table, and the teeth stick out more at the front of the mouth.

Birthday

Horses are aged from 1 January, regardless of when they were born. If a horse's true sixth birthday is 12 April, he is said to be 'rising' 6 between 1 January and 12 April.

Telling the age of a horse

AGE	TEETH
1	Full set of milk incisors. The corners of the top and bottom set do not meet.
2½	Permanent central incisors appear.
3	Permanent central incisors are in use.
3½	Permanent lateral incisors appear.
4	Permanent lateral incisors are in use.
4½	Permanent corners appear.
5	All incisors in use. Tushes have appeared in geldings and some mares.
6	All incisors in use. Tables level and cups dark.
7	Central cups worn out, leaving paler 'mark'. The upper incisors may overlap the lower ones, producing a 'hook' on the back of the upper corner incisors.
8	Lateral cups worn out, leaving paler mark. Centrals have dental star. Hooks worn out.
9	Corner cups worn out, leaving paler mark. Laterals have dental star. Central tables become more triangular.
10	The lower end of Galvayne's groove appears on upper corner incisors, between 9 and 10 years old. On all incisors the marks are less distinct and the dental stars more distinct. Lateral tables become more triangular.
15	Galvayne's groove reaches about halfway down the upper corners.
20	Galvayne's groove reaches the table.
20+	Galvayne's groove's lower end emerges from the gum and gradually moves down until at 25 the upper end has emerged and is clear of the gum.

First aid for horses

First aid box

- Poultice (for use wet or dry)
- Antiseptic spray
- Antiseptic ointment
- Antiseptic cleaning liquid (for cleansing in dilution)
- Crepe bandages
- Self-adhesive bandages
- Cotton wool
- Epsom salts
- Gamgee
- Non-stick dressing
- Peroxide (20% vol)
- Salt
- Veterinary thermometer
- Tweezers
- Scissors
- Petroleum jelly
- Witch hazel
- Sticky back tape (such as silage tape, for fixing foot poultices)
- Eye ointment and eye wash
- Sunblock
- Stethoscope
- Clean bucket or bowl
- Hoof testers

Vital signs

Averages are given for horses at rest. Each horse is different; get to know yours.

Respiration around 12 breaths a minute at rest.

Pulse 36–42 a minute. Slightly more in younger horses.

Temperature 38.5°C (100.5°F). A temperature over 39.5°C (103°F) indicates a serious problem.

Measuring respiration

Stand behind the horse, slightly to one side.

Watch the rise and fall of the flanks.

Count the number of times they rise or fall (one breath is one rise, one fall) in one minute.

If the horse is worried or has just been running or exercising the rate will be higher.

Measuring pulse

The pulse is difficult to find so get some practise.

Try the top of the lower jaw near the throat, the cheek above the level of the eye, the inside fore-leg level with the knee joint.

Press your fingers gently against the pulse.

Count for 30 seconds then double the number.

Measuring temperature

Don't do this alone until you are experienced.

Shake the thermometer until it reads below 37°C (97°F).

Put a little petroleum jelly on the bulb end.

Stand to one side of the horse, raise the dock and insert the thermometer in the rectum, holding it tightly.

After 1–2 minutes withdraw thermometer and take the reading.

Clean and disinfect the thermometer.

digital pulse

Pulse points are indicated left. A digital pulse is only detectable when blood flow into the foot is constricted and it is taken as an indicator of feet problems such as laminitis.

Treating your horse

Small cuts and bruises, mild lameness and minor eye infections may all be treated successfully by an experienced horse keeper. However, many horse ailments will require veterinary attention. Some of the most common problems are described here and the information given should help you to keep your horse comfortable and safe while you wait for the vet's arrival. Other problems are described on pp.28–31.

Mild eye infection

Symptoms

- More tears than usual
- Discharge from eye
- Puffiness in eyelid

Treatment

- Bathe with warm water
- Use a fly mask if the horse is being bothered by flies

Notes

- If symptoms persist or worsen call the vet who may suggest antibiotic eye drops
- If tears are rolling down the cheeks, the tear ducts could be blocked, in which case the vet will need to flush them out
- Where there are signs of damage and/or tenderness, call the vet; while awaiting their arrival, bathe with warm water then use a warm compress to ease the pain

Diarrhoea

Symptoms

- Loose droppings
- Horse becomes sickly
- Weight loss (if prolonged)

Treatment

Identify the cause and treat it accordingly:

- Stress or excitement – the diarrhoea will stop when the horse calms down
- Worm infestation – follow a sensible worming regime (see p.13)
- Recent move to rich pasture – limit the amount of time the horse spends in the pasture or reduce his grazing area
- Poisonous plants or any other suspected poisoning – call the vet immediately
- Bacterial infection, inflammation of the gut – need to be diagnosed and treated by the vet

Colic – abdominal pain

Colic appears more common in stable-kept horses, especially those recently stabled for long periods after being at pasture full time – for example, if they're brought in for box rest. Recent research suggests it may also be brought on by long journeys.

Symptoms – any or all

- Frantic rolling
- Biting or kicking at flanks
- Patchy sweating
- Pawing at ground
- Increased vital signs
- Lying down

Treatment

- Call the vet immediately
- Stable the horse
- Lay a deep bed as protection and to prevent him getting cast
- Keep him warm
- Allow him to drink if he wants to, but do not give any food
- Walk him gently (if recommended by vet) to discourage violent rolling
- Note droppings – loose, hard, or none at all
- If possible, note pulse, temperature and respiration
- Pain-killers, saline, lubricant may all be used by the vet. Twisted gut – a complication of colic – will require immediate surgery.

Choke – food stuck in the throat

Symptoms – any or all

- Coughing after being fed
- Horse very distressed and attempting to swallow
- Nasal discharge
- Increased vital signs
- Swelling visible in throat

Treatment

- Call the vet
- Gently massage the throat to encourage clearance of the blockage

Leg and feet problems

Abscess

Symptoms
- Extreme lameness
- Swelling in lower leg
- Heat in foot
- No obvious wounds or damage

Treatment
- The farrier or vet will use hoof testers to locate the site of the abscess and then dig a hole in the hoof to release the pus and enable the abscess to drain – after which the horse will instantly become much sounder
- Poulticing for 2 days, or until no more dark-coloured pus is seen on the poultice, is usually advised
- Antibiotics are rarely of use

Azoturia

Symptoms
- Hindquarters moving oddly due to swollen, painful muscles
- Profuse sweating and anxiety
- Dark-coloured urine

Treatment
- Call the vet
- Do not make the horse walk, keep him warm by putting a blanket over the quarters
- Prevent reoccurrence by balancing diet with workload (see p.34–37)

Thrush

Symptoms
- Blackness on sole of foot, especially around frog
- Dreadful smell
- Possibly lameness

Treatment
- Clean hooves and scrub away loose, crumbly material
- Disinfect with peroxide solution or purple spray
- Repeat twice daily
- Maintain good stable hygiene

Cuts

- Call a vet if: the wound is bleeding in spurts (a cut artery); the wound is very deep or lacerated, particularly if bone, tendon or other underlying tissue can be seen; clear liquid is visible (joint or tendon fluid); your horse hasn't got a current tetanus vaccination
- Small, shallow, clean cuts that are not bleeding heavily may be treated with antiseptic spray (or cream if the horse dislikes sprays)
- Deep cuts and larger wounds may require stitching (call the vet) and possibly antibiotics. Clean the wound (see below) and try to slow the bleeding; do not use antiseptics until advised by the vet

Cleaning wounds
- Wash your hands
- Get some clean cotton wool and a weak saline or antiseptic solution; with large leg wounds hosing with plain water may be more suitable
- Clean from the centre of the wound outwards
- Clean the surrounding skin
- Use a dressing to stop bleeding if necessary (see 'Fixing a bandage', below); bleeding may take some time to stop

Fixing a bandage
Bandages are usually used only on the legs as they will not stay in place elsewhere
- Place a non-stick dressing over the wound
- Wrap gamgee or other padding around the leg
- From above the wound, leaving an edge of padding visible and working downwards, wrap a bandage around the leg. Leave a margin of padding visible at the bottom, too. Make sure the pressure is even throughout the bandage
- If the dressing is covering a knee or hock, wrap the bandage in a figure of eight to avoid pressure on the joint

Laminitis/founder

Symptoms

- ✦ Lameness – severe or otherwise
- ✦ Heat in the feet
- ✦ Horse tries to stand on its heels, to relieve pain in the hoof

Treatment

- ✦ Call the vet
- ✦ Remove your horse from the source of the problem (see 'Causes of laminitis')
- ✦ Stable your horse on a deep bed
- ✦ Do not feed him until the vet has visited

Causes of laminitis

- ● Obesity
- ● Overfeeding/overeating
- ● Illness, such as Cushing's disease or hormonal imbalances
- ● Drugs, such as corticosteroids
- ● Concussion due to hard road work
- ● Cold weather
- ● Stress
- ● Secondary laminitis may develop when, for example, hindlegs are overworked because the forelegs have laminitis

Lameness

Most lameness (about 9 in 10 cases) occurs due to problems in the feet, such as abcesses, bruising, puncture wounds, which can all benefit from poulticing (see below), and laminitis (left).

Even where the leg is swollen, the cause could be in the foot.

With slight lameness and no obvious swelling or injury, stable the horse for 24 hours and check again – calling the vet if he is still lame.

Intermittent lameness may indicate navicular disease (p.30) or pedal ostitis (p.30).

Tendon sprains, which may occur during turnout or exercise, are characterized by warmth and puffiness around the thickened tendon, as well as varying degrees of lameness – call the vet, cold hose the leg, bandage both it and its partner, then stable your horse until the vet arrives.

Applying a hot foot poultice

- ✦ Clean the foot
- ✦ Cut the poultice to size and shape
- ✦ Place it in warm water then gently squeeze to remove the excess
- ✦ Position the poultice over the sole of the hoof
- ✦ Keep it in place with self-adhesive bandage – wrap the bandage two or three times around the edge of the hoof first then gradually cover the poultice by bringing the bandage over the sole and around the hoof wall working up the hoof to the coronet, making sure you do not make it too tight when you reach the coronet
- ✦ Use a poultice boot or layers of sticky back tape to keep the whole thing in place (especially if the horse has to go back out into a field)

First aid for people

First aid box

Choose a clean waterproof container, mark it clearly and put it in an obvious place.

- A selection of individually wrapped adhesive dressings and plasters
- Sterile dressings
- Bandages – rolled and triangular
- Cotton wool – for padding only
- Wound cleasing wipes – alcohol-free
- Safety pins, scissors, tweezers
- Thermometer
- Torch, blanket, whistle

Vital signs

Respiration 12–16 breaths per minute in adults, 20–30 in babies and young children.

Pulse 60–80 per minute in adults, less in very fit people, more in babies.

Temperature 37°C (98.6°F).

Calling an ambulance

You will need to tell emergency services:

- ✔ Your exact location and clear directions to it
- ✔ What has happened and who is involved
- ✔ Your name and phone number

Important note

Riding is a risk sport but you can make it safer for yourself and others by being aware of the risks and how to deal with any incidents. Please go out and buy yourself a good first aid manual (authorized by a well-known first aid provider such as St John's Ambulance, St Andrew's Ambulance Association or the British Red Cross), get to know the book well, especially the basic first aid procedures, and then keep it readily to hand. Better still, go on a first aid course – you could save a life.

Shock

Symptoms
- ✦ Rapid pulse
- ✦ Cold skin, blue-tinged around the mouth
- ✦ Sweating
- ✦ Weakness
- ✦ Possibly leading to a weakened pulse and unconsciousness

Treatment
- ✦ Deal with any injuries
- ✦ Lie casualty down
- ✦ Raise their legs if possible
- ✦ Loosen tight clothing
- ✦ Keep them warm with a blanket
- ✦ Call an ambulance

Concussion

Symptoms
- ✦ Short-lived loss of consciousness
- ✦ Dizziness or nausea
- ✦ Memory loss
- ✦ Mild headache

Treatment
- ✦ If unconscious, follow the procedure outlined in 'Unconscious injured casualty' (opposite)
- ✦ If the casualty seems conscious, ensure they remain lying down, or sitting, until they can respond sensibly to questions and feel pain – a pinch
- ✦ If headache, nausea, vomiting, excessive drowsiness occur the casualty must be taken to hospital

Severe bleeding

Treatment
- ✦ Clear the wound of clothing
- ✦ Use a dressing and your hand to apply pressure to the wound
- ✦ Raise the wound – lie the casualty down
- ✦ Leaving the dressing in place, bandage the wound – not so tight that it restricts blood circulation
- ✦ Call an ambulance

Eye injury
Treatment
✦The casualty should be taken to hospital lying down – call an ambulance if your car is unsuitable
✦Tell them to keep their head and the uninjured eye still (this keeps the injured eye still too)
✦Give them a clean dressing or other protection to put over the eye

Spinal injury
Symptoms
✦Pain or tenderness in neck or back
✦Limbs weak or unable to move
✦Breathing difficulties
✦Loss of bladder or bowel control

Treatment
✦Keep the head and neck still and supported
✦Call an ambulance

Broken bones
Symptoms
✦Bruising and distortion
✦Pain, especially when the limb is moved

Treatment
✦Protect the break as far as possible
✦Call an ambulance

Skull fracture
If there is severe bleeding from a head wound, the skull may also be damaged, this might be indicated by a loss of consciousness (even if only very short-lived). Clear liquid or watery blood leaking from an ear or the nose point to a severe head injury. Lie the casualty down and call an ambulance immediately.

Unconscious injured casualty
These points are a guide only, they are not a substitute for proper first-aid training. Where an unconscious person is not injured and not breathing the most likely cause is a heart attack – call an ambulance immediately.

●**Do not move the person** unless they are in danger where they are; don't remove their riding hat.

●**If the person is breathing**, put them in the recovery position (below left), unless you suspect a serious neck injury, and call an ambulance.

●**If the person is not breathing:**

Ensure that they can breathe by opening their airway – lie them on their back and tilt their head gently backwards (you may have to undo the chinstrap), open their mouth and carefully remove any obvious obstruction. Lift the chin.

●**If they don't immediately breathe on their own:**

Carry out rescue breaths – use one hand to pinch their nose closed, use the other to hold their chin, take a deep breath, place your mouth over their mouth, blow steadily until their chest rises (about 2 seconds), remove your mouth, check that their chest falls. Repeat this procedure once more, then check whether the casualty is breathing. If they are put them in the recovery position (below left) and call an ambulance.

If the casualty is still not breathing:

●Carry out CPR (cardiopulmonary resuscitation) and rescue breaths – kneeling beside them, place the heel of one hand on their breastbone, place your other hand on top and interlock the fingers, leaning over the casualty, with arms straight, press down vertically, depressing their chest by 4–5cm (1½–2in), release the pressure without removing your hands. Compress and release the chest 15 times quite quickly (at a rate of 100 compressions every 60 seconds). Now give two rescue breaths (as described above).

●If the casualty starts to breathe on their own, put them in the recovery position. If not, repeat the procedure described for one minute before calling for an ambulance. Continue with the procedure until help arrives.

Horse health

This is a brief guide to some of the problems that horses may experience. Unless you are absolutely sure what is wrong with your horse and are completely confident you can treat it yourself, you should always seek professional help.

Abscess Pus formed in the foot, causing extreme lameness, or under the skin in response to an infection. Antibiotics are sometimes used except in the cases of foot abscesses (see p.24) and **strangles**.

Arthritis (degenerative joint disease, DJD) This is inflammation in a joint or joints. Acute arthritis occurs due to a wound or infection; it causes heat and swelling and needs immediate treatment, including antibiotics and joint immoblization. Chronic arthritis develops more slowly and is often caused by repeated work-related stress on the joints; slower to develop, it produces stiffness and lameness. Although there is no cure, the symptoms can be relieved through gentle in-hand exercise, the use of anti-inflammatories (bute), and other drugs, including corticosteroids.

Aural plaques Crusty white scabs form inside the ear and the skin beneath is sensitive, pink and thickened. There is no completely successful treatment but bathing with anti-inflammatories will reduce the size of the plaques.

Azoturia See p.24.

Bog spavin See Bursal strains and injuries.

Botulism poisoning An often fatal poisoning, associated with eating infected food, such as soil-contaminated silage. Botulism causes muscle paralysis and respiratory failure. Symptoms appear about 4–5 days after infection: the horse has trouble eating and moving; he may stand with his head lowered.

Bruised sole A common cause of lameness, especially in the front feet. In white-footed horses bruising can be seen as a discoloured area; hoof-testers will also reveal sensitivity. Rest the horse, protecting the bruised foot, for 7–10 days. See also **Corns**.

Bursal strains and injuries (bursitis) Damage to the bursae (sacs) around bony areas, such as joints, causes over-production of the lubricating synovial fluid they contain, and this shows as soft swelling – called a bursal enlargement. Windgalls, bog spavins and thoroughpins are bursal strains. They are not very serious but may be initially painful. Treatment includes rest, cold hosing and massage. Capped hocks, elbows and knees are bursal injuries and are often painless, although it is sometimes advisable to drain the fluid from the area and apply a pressure bandage to prevent more building up.

Capped elbow/capped hock See Bursal strains and injuries.

Choke See p.23.

COPD (chronic obstructive pulmonary disease, heaves) A respiratory disease characterized by a hollow cough and reduced performance. It is caused by allergies, usually to mould spores in hay or straw, and possibly also pollen. A vet will treat symptoms then preventative measures, such as good stable hygiene, keeps COPD under control.

Colic See p.23.

Corns A cause of lameness, these are bruises at the heel of the foot and may result from infrequent shoeing or poor trimming. **Abscesses** may also develop in the area. Regular good quality farriery required. See also **Bruised sole**.

Curb A strain of the tendon at the back of the hock, indicated by a firm, perhaps warm swelling about 10cm (4in) below the point of hock, and possibly slight lameness in the early stages. A vet will treat inflammation; rest usually results in complete recovery.

Cushing's disease This is caused by a tumour on the pituitary gland, which affects hormone production. Symptoms include increased thirst and urination, the development of a long, persistent curly coat, and a sway back and pot-belly. There is an increased proneness to laminitis and mouth ulcers, and healing of cuts becomes slower. No cure. A vet will suggest treatment to relieve symptoms and a good diet can help.

Dehydration Indicated by tight dry skin and depression. Dehydration can occur due to heavy sweating or as a result of diarrhoea. Water and electrolytes should stabilize the horse. If dehydration has not obviously been caused by workload call your vet immediately.

Endometritis An infection in mares (developed during foaling or because of an infected stallion) indicated by a persistent cloudy vulval discharge and a high temperature, possibly also laminitis and endotoxic shock. It also occurs due to a deformed vulva that allows air along with faecal contaminents to be drawn into the vagina (vulval aspiration); in this case a surgical procedure (Caslick's operation or Pouret's operation) is needed. See also **Endotoxaemia**.

Endotoxaemia An often fatal condition caused when bacteria from the intestines get into the rest of the horse's system, because of other problems such as colitis, twisted gut, concentrate overload. Indicators include depression, increased pulse rate, dehydration, colic-like symptoms, diarrhoea, excessive drinking.

Equine herpes virus (EHV) A series of viruses that cause respiratory, reproductive and neurological problems and spread mainly through the copious nasal discharge produced by infected animals. Incubation takes up to 10 days and horses may take 3 months to recover fully. Short-lived preventative vaccinations can be given; the viruses cannot be treated although some of the symptoms can be relieved with antibiotics and good nursing.

Equine infectious anaemia (EIA) A persistent virus initially causing fever, anaemia, body oedema and lethargy. Then recovery appears to take place but a few weeks later fluctuating periods of fever occur. Full recovery takes about a year but the horse has become a carrier. Coggins test diagnoses the disease; no treatment is available.

Equine influenza Most horses are vaccinated against equine flu, a serious respiratory disease (sometimes fatal in youngstock) causing high temperatures, clear nasal discharge and coughing. Incubation takes 3–4 days and recovery about 3 weeks. Treatment includes prolonged rest along with drug therapy. Recovered horses may be carriers.

Filled legs Horses kept stabled for long periods can suffer from poor circulation leading to swelling in the legs due to lymph escaping into surrounding tissues, rather than being circulated back up the legs. Increased turnout, a more roomy stable and stable bandages can help. It may degenerate into **lymphangitis**.

Head shaker A horse that shakes its head when ridden. Shaking is usually persistent; it may be mild or excessive. The cause may be nerve pain, and is often exacerbated by well known irritants such as pollen or dust. Full or partial facial nets are useful in many cases; drugs or surgery may help in others. Head shaking can also be caused by other physical problems, such as uncomfortable teeth.

Laminitis See p.25.

Locking patella This is where the stay mechanism that allows horses to doze while standing seizes up causing the leg to drag when the horse moves – it usually frees itself within minutes. It is a condition that often affects horses in poor health and disappears when they regain health. Surgery is sometimes required.

Lymphangitis Infection in the lymph vessels and tissues of the lower (usually hind) legs, causing hot and painful swelling and lameness. Liquid may ooze from the skin. Lymphangitis may be a complication of **mud fever**, **filled legs** or an untreated injury. Diuretics and anti-inflammatories are used to relieve it.

Mud fever (greasy heel) Inflammation and scabs on the heels and fetlocks caused by bacteria gaining entry through skin softened by being constantly wet and muddy. The pastern and fetlock may become swollen. Treatment includes cleansing the lower legs and using antibiotic ointment; barrier creams may help in prevention.

Navicular disease A degenerative disorder of the tiny navicular bone in the front feet. Symptoms include tripping and a gradual change of gait and onset of lameness. Drug therapies, surgery and remedial shoeing can relieve the symptoms.

Nose bleeds Bleeding from one or both nostrils after strenuous exercise. Bleeding may also be undetected as the blood goes down the trachea and is swallowed. Treatment is not always successful, although treatment of other respiratory problems can help, as can good stable hygiene.

Pedal ostitis Inflammation of the pedal bone of the front feet, leading to lameness. Anti-inflammatories and remedial shoeing can ease the symptoms.

Poisoning As horses are quite fussy eaters, they are very rarely poisoned. However, certain circumstances, such as food shortage, a huge fresh supply of the poisonous plant or it being present dried in forage, will sometimes lead them to eat what they would normally avoid. There are many forms of poisoning and few specific treatments (one example is dosing with thiamine to counteract bracken and mare's tail poisoning: these plants destroy this enzyme in the body), often the only recourse is to treat the symptoms and, unfortunately, the outcome is frequently death. (See also 'Poisonous plants', opposite and p.40.)

Rainscald (**weather beat**) Similar to **mud fever** except that it affects the body, rainscald is characterized by scabby areas on the back or neck, under which the skin is red and sore. In mild cases regular grooming will remove the problem, otherwise shampooing and antibiotic creams will be required. Antibiotics may be needed in severe cases.

Ringbone Slow-growing bony swelling on the pastern bones caused by concussion or injury. Where it restricts the action of the joints, it generally leads to long-term lameness; between the joints it often resolves after rest and treatment. Anti-inflammatory drugs and surgery may be required.

Ringworm Highly contagious disease (in people as well as animals) characterized by round, raised areas on the skin that grow and spread, bursting and becoming scabby. A vet will prescribe systemic antibiotics; antibiotic skin washes may also be used.

Sarcoid Tumour that can be likened to cancer, except that it affects only the skin. Sarcoids may be caused by viruses, but do not appear contagious. A damaged sarcoid can become aggressive and start growing and spreading more quickly, which makes biopsies or half-hearted attempts at treatment a risk. If the sarcoid is 'quiet' and not in a place where it might cause problems (such as under the saddle), it may be best left alone. If treatment is decided upon, it must be carried out under a vet's guidance, with careful monitoring at all stages. Treatment may include surgical removal or freezing of the sarcoid, radiation treatment or the use of highly toxic ointments.

Sand cracks See p.45.

Seedy toe See p.45.

Sesamoiditis Disease in or damage to the sesamoid bones, which causes pain and swelling at the back of the fetlock joint and lameness. A vet will prescribe long rest (up to a year) and anti-inflammatory drugs.

Spavin Causing lameness in the hindlegs, this is a form of **arthritis** affecting the small bones in the hock.

Splint A hard swelling between the cannon and splint bones, often on the front legs, in young horses. As they form, they may be warm and cause lameness, but mature splints are cold and rarely cause trouble. Rest and anti-inflammatory treatment usually recommended.

Strangles A highly contagious infection of the upper respiratory tract causing raised temperature, nasal discharge, loss of appetite and swelling around the jaw due to **abscesses** in the throat. Infected horses must be isolated for at least 3 weeks. Hot poulticing helps the abscesses to drain. A vet will confirm the disease and recommend suitable treatment. Antibiotics are rarely used.

Stringhalt Horses affected by stringhalt have an odd hindleg action, lifting the legs over-high and slamming them down hard. In some countries, dandelion poisoning may be implicated. Muscle relaxants can be an effective treatment; surgery is sometimes used.

Sweet itch An allergic reaction to midge saliva, sweet itch causes the affected horse to rub itself raw on the mane and/or tail. Barrier rugs stop the midges getting to the skin and their use can be combined with fly repellents. Corticosteroids can be used, but have side effects, including increased proneness to laminitis.

Thoroughpin See Bursal strains and injuries.

Thrush See p.24.

Uveitis (moonblindness) This disease affects the inside and outside of the eye, as well as the surrounding tissues, and is extremely painful for the horse. The pupil constricts and the eye becomes very sensitive to light. Copious tears are produced, and the eyelids, which are inflammed, tend to be fast-closed. The cause may be bacteria or worm larvae; treatment includes antibiotics, corticosteroids and atropine. The problem tends to reoccur and eventually leads to blindness.

Urticaria (hives) Lumps appearing on the skin in association with swollen facial features and legs are a sign of an allergic reaction, usually to a change of diet or an insect bite. Antihistamine or corticosteroids are administered by the vet to relieve the symptoms.

Warts Small warts appear on the thin-skinned areas of a horse, such as the nostrils or eyelids. They usually occur in young horses and will grow, changing from grey to reddish, then drop off. Although they can be removed by the vet, they will disappear of their own accord after 3–4 months.

Windgalls See Bursal strains and injuries.

some more common poisonous plants

yew

hemlock

acorn

buttercup

ragwort

ivy

Road safety

Advice to riders

✔ Wear a hard hat when riding on the road; in Britain children under 14 years old must wear one, otherwise their parents may face prosecution (see p.7).

✔ Wear high visibility gear (tabards or leg and arm bands) even in summer, when shadows or the sun can prevent drivers seeing you.

✔ Be courteous to drivers and other road users, even if they are not courteous in return – next time they might be.

✔ Get third party insurance so if you are involved in an accident you are covered for any damage you or your horse do.

✔ Learn the Highway Code/Vehicle Code and, in Britain, take your BHS Riding and Safety Road Test (see 'By law', below right).

✔ If you or your horse are inexperienced or nervous of traffic, ride on the road only during calm periods and always with a calm escort.

✔ Never take risks – if your horse is scared of something on the road, wait until all is clear before passing.

✔ If safety dictates, ride a little out from the curb to be more visible or to prevent cars passing where it might be dangerous.

✔ Don't ride on icy roads.

Advice to drivers

✔ Give horses a wide berth and pass slowly – remember, they are not like cars, they can leap sideways into the road if something on the roadside startles them.

✔ Drive slowly on country roads and lanes – horses, walkers and other slow traffic might be just around the corner.

✔ If you are behind a horse and a vehicle is approaching in the opposite direction, wait for it to pass before passing the horse.

Roadcraft

✔ Ask a driver to slow down by stretching your arm out, palm down, then raising and lowering your arm.

✔ Ask a driver to stop by raising your hand, palm out towards the driver.

✔ Use your arm to indicate clearly which way you are turning.

✔ Before making any manoeuvre Look, Listen, Observe, Look Again – this is the Life-saver Look.

✔ Whatever way you are turning, stay by the kerb until the road is clear.

✔ On roundabouts keep by the kerb until you reach your turning.

✔ Obey road signs and traffic lights.

Driver, slow down or stop

Driver, stop

I intend to turn right

I intend to turn left

By law

● You must not ride on a pedestrian path or pavement.

● In the UK and parts of the USA, you must wear a hard hat if you are under 14.

Trailers and horse boxes

Before loading ask yourself*:

Is the trailer or lorry appropriate for my horse?

✔ Check capacity (see 'MAM').
✔ Check internal size – there should be space for your horse to stand easily without restriction, and allow at least 20cm (8in) above his natural head height.
✔ Make sure it's clean and well ventilated.
✔ Check the floor is non-slip and any partitions are fitted properly.
✔ Is it safe (see also Insurance)?
✔ Check the flooring, the condition of the towbar, the state of the wheels, the lights.

Is my vehicle appropriate for towing?

✔ It must be capable of towing the combined weight of the trailer and its maximum load (indicated in the handbook, or check with the manufacturer).
✔ The combined weight of the trailer and its maximum load should be less than 85% of the actual weight of the towing vehicle.
✔ 4-wheel drives are best for towing trailers as they cope better with hills and off-road driving.
✔ Check oil, water, tyre pressure; keep the vehicle well maintained.
✔ Carry a fire extinguisher, a breakdown triangle and a torch.

Am I safe?

✔ In Britain, if you passed your driving test after 1st January 1997 your MAM is 3,500kg – usually easily exceeded by a tow vehicle, let alone the trailer. Take an additional driving test to be legal.
✔ If you passed your driving test before 1st January 1997 but are inexperienced at towing, you owe it to your horse to take an additional driving test.
✔ If you're a bit rusty, practise reversing and pulling away with the trailer empty.
✔ Take a mobile phone – remember your breakdown assistance numbers and card – and something fluorescent to wear in the event of a breakdown. It is preferable to take someone with you to help if necessary.
✔ Make sure you know how to change a tyre.
(*Obviously, some of these points only relate to trailers.)

MAM/MGW

Maximum authorized mass, or maximum gross weight, indicates the loading capacity of a trailer or lorry. The MAM is usually indicated on a manufacturer's plate on the vehicle, often on the towbar on trailers. Never exceed this figure.

Towing Ability Test

In Britain you can find out where to do a towing ability test by contacting an approved driving instructor. Or, contact trailer manufacturers who will be able to help.

Insurance

Your insurance will be invalidated if:
✘ your vehicle is not appropriate for pulling your trailer.
✘ you are not licensed to tow a trailer.
✘ you exceed the MAM.

Long journeys

✔ Provide a deep bed.
✔ Feed and water at least every 6–8 hours.
✔ Allow space for foals and young horses to lie down on journeys of more than 12 hours.
✔ Plan ahead for stops where horses can be unloaded and rested with shelter from the weather.

Know the law

The Equine Law and Horsemanship Safety website (www.utexas.edu/dawson), set up and maintained by the University of Texas and the AAHS (American Association for Horsemanship Safety), details laws affecting horses and horse riders in the USA, along with lots of other useful information.

Feeding your horse

Feeding facts

- Horses like to eat for 16–20 hours a day.
- A grass-kept horse can eat 2–3kg (4–6½lbs) of grass an hour, which means up to 60kg (132¼lb) a day.
- A horse can eat about 2.5% of its total weight daily – this is its total appetite.
- Sufficient roughage is vital in maintaining a healthy horse; balance between roughage and concentrate is also vital (see 'How much forage?' p.37).
- Good quality concentrate mixes (sweet feeds) are nutritionally balanced – choose the correct energy level and feed the amounts suggested, and you shouldn't need to feed supplements; if you feed less than the recommended levels (see 'Feed Chart', p.36), consider including a broad spectrum supplement.
- Always alter a horse's diet gradually to give the bacteria in his gut time to adjust.
- A horse requires up to 55 litres (12 gallons) of water a day.
- Salt should always be available to your horse – usually in the form of a salt lick, but don't put it near the water trough.
- Overfeeding concentrates will exaggerate a horse's natural behaviour but cannot change his character.

Some definitions

- **Lignin** – woody fibres in plant material, these cannot be digested by the horse.
- **Cellulose** – slightly less woody than lignin, these can be digested.
- **Cereal concentrates** – grains such as oats, wheat, barley, maize, corn.
- **Non-cereal concentrates** – sugar beet, alfalfa, beans, peas, linseed, soya beans.
- **MJ (megajoule)** – a unit of energy equivalent to 240 calories.
- **DE (digestible energy)** – the energy the horse can actually get out of the food.
- **Electrolytes** – also called tissue salts, these are sodium, potassium, chlorine and they regulate body fluids.

Nutrition

These ingredients make up a horse's diet:

- ✦ **Carbohydrate**, about two-thirds of the diet, is the main provider of heat and energy.
- ✦ **Protein**, about one sixth of the diet, is for body tissue repair and muscle development.
- ✦ **Oil/fat**, about one sixth of the horse's diet, provides more heat and energy, but more slowly, than the same amount of carbohydrate (it has 35mj de/kg); however, it is fed in smaller quantities. It conditions skin, hair, horn.
- ✦ **Fibre** is found in the food that provides protein and carbohydrate and is essential for a healthy gut.
- ✦ **Vitamins and minerals** are required in very small quantities, overdoses can be as dangerous as deficiencies.
- ✦ **Water** is essential for all life.

What does your horse weigh?

The easiest way to find out what your horse weighs is with a weigh tape. These are cheap, widely available, simple to use and reasonably accurate. Otherwise, you can estimate using the following formula:

$$\text{weight (kgs)} = \frac{\textbf{girth} \times \textbf{length} \times \textbf{length}}{11{,}000}$$

(Note: girth is the circumference of the horse just behind its front legs, length is from point of shoulder to point of buttocks. Remember to use centimetres.)

Table of weights

This table gives only a very rough guide to weight as so much depends on the horse's build – even if they are both the same height, a slight thoroughbred is likely to be somewhat lighter than a heavily built cob.

height	weight
10hh	to 190kg (419lb)
11hh	to 200kg (440lb)
12hh	to 300kg (660lb)
13hh	to 350kg (772lb)
14hh	to 400kg (882lb)
14.2hh	to 450kg (992lb)
15–15.2hh	to 500kg (1,102lb)
16–16.2hh	to 550kg (1,212lb)
17–17.2hh	to 600kg (1,323lb)

Vitamins and minerals

The vitamins a horse requires are:

Vitamin A for eyesight, mucous membranes and skin health. Vitamin A is readily available in good summer pasture. Feed carrots and oil in winter to boost vitamin A levels.

Vitamin B-group necessary for red blood cell formation and a balanced metabolism. Gut activity from a high fibre diet produces vitamin B. Horses in hard work may benefit from a supplement.

Vitamin C for tissue health and to aid disease defence mechanisms. It is usually produced in sufficient quantities by a healthy digestive system, although stressed horses may benefit from a supplement.

Vitamin D for bone formation. Sunlight enables a horse to produce its own vitamin D. Feed oil in winter to overcome deficiencies caused by lack of sunlight.

Vitamin E for a healthy immune system and red blood cell production. It is usually freely available in good pastures and from concentrates.

Vitamin K is stored by the horse and usually freely available in good pasture.

The major minerals a horse requires are:

Calcium (Ca), **phosphorus (P)** with vitamin D for bone maintenance.

Magnesium (Mg) for bone structure and to activate enzymes.

Sulphur (S) for the production of enzymes, hormones and amino acids.

Sodium (Na), **potassium (K)**, **chloride (Cl)** for regulating body fluids.

Potassium is found in forage, the other major minerals are usually provided in sufficient quantities in good quality feeds.

The trace minerals a horse requires are:

Copper (Cu), **iron (Fe)** to aid blood formation

Selenium (Se) with vitamin E for muscle strength.

Cobalt (Co), **iodine (I)**, **manganese (Mn)**, **zinc (Zn)**.

Trace minerals are all usually provided in sufficient quanties in good quality feeds.

Does your horse need supplements?

◆ How old is your horse? Older horses are less able to absorb vitamins and minerals; youngsters may need additional vitamins or minerals, as might mares in foal.

◆ How is he kept? Stabled horses are more likely to be deficient than grass-kept ones.

◆ How much work does he get? A high-performance horse will require more vitamins and minerals than a horse kept for light hacking.

◆ How good is the pasture? Some soils and, therefore, the grasses growing on them are deficient in minerals such as potassium, iron, zinc, sulphur, selenium.

◆ How good is your forage? Hay and haylage made in areas where the soil is deficient may also be deficient.

A label on a typical mixed concentrate feed

An analysis of the nutrients:

In the European Union, bags of concentrated feed (sweet feed) must indicate the dry weight percentage they contain of each nutrient, except carbohydrate but including the types and amounts of vitamins and minerals. Ash is any inorganic material other than protein, oil and carbohydrate; this indicates the percentage of vitamins and minerals:

Oil 4.0%
Protein 12.0%
Fibre 11.0%
Ash 7.5%
Moisture 14.4%
Vitamin A 14025 i.u./kg; Vitamin D3 1500 i.u./kg; Vitamin E 207 i.u./kg; Selenium 0.43 mg/kg; Copper 44 mg/kg

A best before date:

If you feed after this date the quality and quantity of vitamins and minerals present may have declined.

A list of ingredients:

The ingredients are listed in descending order by weight; this means that feed is made up of mostly the first few items; the last few items (usually the vitamins and minerals) are only present in tiny quantities.

Feed Chart

This chart shows the total number of mega-joules (mj) of digestible energy (de) required by horses of various sizes in various types of work. As it is vital to feed the correct ratio of forage to concentrate (see 'How much forage?', p.37), the chart also shows the number of megajoules required from forage and from concentrate, assuming that the forage contains 7mj de/kg (reasonable quality hay) and the concentrate contains 12mj de/kg (an average concentrate/

sweet feed mix). Beneath these figures are shown the weight required of each, so, for example, a 200kg horse in light work requires 4.5kg of forage and 850gm of concentrate a day. The chart will, therefore, give a rough idea of how much you should feed your horse and in what proportion; it should also be fairly easy to work out how much more or less you should feed as his weight or work varies. Before working out a ration, read the notes below.

Horse weight (kg)	Light work total mj = forage + concentrate	Medium work total mj = forage + concentrate	Hard work total mj = forage + concentrate
200	42= 32 + 10 = 4.5 + 0.85	50 = 25 + 25 = 3.5 + 2	58 = 15 + 43 = 2 + 3.5
250	48 = 36 + 12 = 5 + 1	58 = 29 + 29 = 4 + 2.5	68 = 17 + 51 = 2.5 + 4.25
300	54 = 41 + 13 = 6 + 1.1	66 = 33 + 33 = 4.75 + 2.75	78 = 20 + 58 = 3 + 5
350	60 = 45 + 15 = 6.5 + 1.25	74 = 37 + 37 = 5.25 + 3	88 = 22 + 66 = 3 + 5.5
400	66 = 50 + 16 = 7 + 1.3	82 = 41 + 41 = 6 + 3.5	98 = 25 + 73 = 3.5 + 6
450	72 = 54 + 18 = 7.75 + 1.5	90 = 45 + 45 = 6.5 + 3.75	108 = 27 + 81 = 4 + 6.75
500	78 = 59 + 19 = 8.5 + 1.6	98 = 49 + 49 = 7 + 4	118 = 30 + 88 = 4.25 + 7.25
550	84 = 63 + 21 = 9 + 1.75	106 = 53 + 53 = 7.5 + 4.5	128 = 32 + 96 = 4.5 + 8
600	90 = 68 + 22 = 9.75 + 1.8	114 = 57 + 57 = 8 + 4.75	138 = 34 + 103 = 5 + 8.5
	1 hour walking daily	walking, trotting and some cantering daily	1-day event/training or competing

Notes:
- This chart is a guide only – monitor your horse's weight, work level and performance and be prepared to adjust how much you feed as necessary.
- All horses are different, some will do very well on very little, while others need more to stay in condition.
- Remember that a horse at grass will eat almost continually – grass contains around 2.5mj de/kg (see 'Feeding facts', p.34). Take this into account in your calculations.
- The chart assumes that the horse is the correct weight to begin with. If weight loss or weight gain is required, feed slightly more or slightly less, remembering that a horse has a finite appetite (see 'Feeding facts', p.34).

Relative weights:
A slice of hay = 2kg
A scoop of cubes = 1.5kg
A scoop of concentrate (sweet feed) = 1kg
A double handful of chaff = 250g
A glop of oil = 100g

Ingredients in concentrate mixes (sweet feeds)

These are some of the ingredients used in concentrates. None should be fed in isolation.

Oats – bruised, crushed or rolled; reasonably high in fibre compared to other cereals; have a reputation for making horses fizzy, perhaps because they are easily digested, making the energy they contain quickly available. 11–12mj de/kg.

Barley – bruised, crushed or rolled; cannot be fed whole unless boiled. 12–13mj de/kg.

Wheat – usually micronized or as bran; high fibre content. 12–13mj de/kg.

Maize – usually flaked or otherwise processed; higher energy content than oats or barley, but processing reduces this. 14–15mj de/kg.

Sugar beet – high energy source, but slow-release; rich in salt. If fed separately, it is best to feed the unmolassed variety; molasses encourage a horse to eat much faster and the molassed type may be 40% molasses. 10.5mj de/kg.

Soya beans – cooked or processed; very protein rich, even as soya bean meal, which has had the oil extracted. 13–15mj de/kg.

Peas – cooked or processed; very protein rich. 14mj de/kg.

Forage

● **Hay** – grass cut and dried when mature and stalky so much of the nutrient content is trapped in the stalks as indigestible lignin. Meadow hay contains a variety of grasses – rye grass, cocksfoot, timothy – along with some clover and herbs. Seed hay is made from a specially grown grass crop, usually rye grass. Seed hay is more nutritious than meadow hay, lighter in colour and feels harder when you touch it. Soak all hay before feeding it. 7–9mj de/kg depending on quality.

● **Haylage** – grass cut and partially dried then vacuum-packed so it ferments. Often highly nutritious, but eaten almost twice as quickly as hay – 1kg (2lb) of haylage takes about 12 minutes to eat while 1kg (2lb) of hay takes about 20 minutes. Also, because haylage contains more water than hay, more of it by weight, must be fed. About 6mj de/kg.

● **Silage** – pickled grass, best not fed to horses as there is the risk of botulism (see p.28) and contamination from soil. High protein content.

● **Oat straw** – the stalky by-product of harvesting oats. Provides additional roughage; most of its nutrients are trapped in the lignin. Wheat and barley straws are not really suitable for feeding. Oat straw 8mj de/kg; barley staw 7mj de/kg.

● **Grass** – this is sold dried for horses with respiratory problems and other dietary needs. It is very nutritious but also expensive. Good mixed with cereal feed to balance out deficiencies. About 2.5mj de/kg growing, 10mj de/kg when dried.

● **Alfalfa/lucerne** – dried or in a molassed chaff form. Good mixed with cereal feed to balance out deficiencies. It is high in protein, calcium, vitamins and minerals. About 9mj de/kg.

How much forage?

These figures are by weight for mature horses.

Resting – wholly forage

Light to medium work – ¾ forage ¼ concentrate

Medium – ½ forage ½ concentrate

Hard work – up to ¼ forage ¾ concentrate

Perfect pastures

Some definitions

- **Harrowing** – removal of matted dead grass by means of a chain harrow pulled by a 4-wheel drive, ATV or tractor. Done in late winter or early spring it will also improve poached areas, especially if the field is rolled afterwards.
- **Leaching** – an effect similar to rinsing. Many fertilizers are leached out of the soil by rain, meaning they end up in local waterways and are no longer available to grasses and other plants.
- **pH** – the measurement of acidity and alkalinity. pH 7 is neutral, lower than that is acid (eg pH 6), higher is alkaline (eg pH 7.5). Soil pH affects grass growth (see 'Know your soil').
- **Poaching** – muddy rutted conditions that develop where drainage is poor or where animals congregate.
- **Tillering** – the formation of small shoots at the base of the grass, enabling it to spread.
- **Topping** – mowing grass at a high setting to remove tall and/or rank growth and weeds.

Paddock care

- ✦ Ideally, divide land into 3 paddocks: one being used, one being renovated (weed-killing, reseeding, fertilizing, harrowing), one growing.
- ✦ Consider improving drainage. Good drainage vastly improves pasture and is well worth the initial expense.
- ✦ Where complete renovation is required, use cattle to eat the pasture bare, harrow, seed and roll, then graze lightly with sheep. After this rest until there is even growth throughout the paddock.

Weedkilling

Consider spot weedkilling or digging up nuisance plants, such as docks and thistles, rather than wholesale spraying, which is less environmentally friendly and will kill off herbs and other plants that horses really enjoy eating (see 'Herbs', p.40).

Assessing pasture

- ✦ Boundaries – are they safe (see 'Considering boundaries', below right)?
- ✦ Clean – is the field mostly clear of manure and rough patches of grass?
- ✦ Convenient – is it easy to access the field, are approaches easy, is parking safe?
- ✦ Gates – are they secure, do they open into the field (safer)? Is allowance made for poaching in winter? Mesh or stone topping reduce poaching.
- ✦ Grass quality – is there plenty of grass, few weeds, no poisonous plants? Indicators of poor grazing include horsetails, thistles, bracken, docks, rushes and sedges, damp areas.
- ✦ Shelter – is there shelter (even if only trees or banks), is it enough for all the horses to use, is it sheltered from prevailing weather, is it sufficiently well-drained to avoid poaching?
- ✦ Size – is there at least 0.4ha (1 acre) available for each horse, with the possibility of rotation to rest the paddocks?
- ✦ Suitability – is it a good pasture for your horse? Does he need restricted grazing or particularly good fencing? Can this be arranged?
- ✦ Water – is the supply clean, constant and within easy reach? Are the troughs safe for horses – no sharp corners?

Horse manure

- ✔ Pick up daily or every other day to maximize areas for eating.
- ✔ Spread on fields (if necessary) when well rotted – preferably at least 1 year.
- ✔ Spread in autumn on paddocks due for winter resting and spring on the winter paddocks.
- ✔ Keep horses off for 6 months to prevent parasite infestation (see 'Worms and worming', p.40).
- ✔ Harrowing instead of poo-picking simply spreads the worm eggs but can be done if the field is then well rested (eg for hay) or cross grazed (1 cow/6 sheep an 0.4ha/acre).

Know your soil

Sandy soil
✦ Good drainage, not so likely to poach.
✦ Remains good for riding on year-round.
✦ Warms up quickly in spring, so grass growth starts early.
✦ Grows poor grass, particularly in summer.
✦ Needs regular fertilization.
✦ Benefits from addition of organic matter, such as farmyard manure.

Clay soil
✦ Cold, so grass growth is slow to start in spring.
✦ Grows good grass.
✦ Gets very hard in summer, deep and muddy in winter.
✦ Only suitable for riding on in spring/autumn.
✦ Likely to be reasonably fertile.
✦ Benefits from drainage work.

Acid/alkaline?
✦ Ideal pH is 6.5. Simple soil testing kits are sold at garden centres – test several sample areas. Some fertilizer companies will carry out soil analysis, which will also tell you whether other nutrients are low (see 'Inorganic fertilizers').
✦ Improve alkaline soil by adding farmyard manure, which is acid, in autumn or winter. Keep horses off for at least two months.
✦ Improve acid soil by liming (basic slag will also provide phosphates, see 'Inorganic fertilizers') – up to 5,000kg per ha (2 tons per acre) in autumn or winter (every 5–8 years). Keep horses off until rain has washed it in.
✦ Any improvements are short-lived so regular testing and improving is required.

Using fertilizers

Inorganic fertilizers
These include nitrogen, phosphorus (phosphate) and potassium (potash), all necessary for plant growth and health.

Phosphorus
✦ Encourages clover, which improves nitrogen content (see 'Pasture plants', p.41)
✦ Use with care as it can upset horse's calcium:phosphorus balance (see p.35)
✦ Where required, apply it every 2–3 years

Potassium
✦ Likely to be deficient in lime-rich soils
✦ Not easily leached out by rain
✦ Annual dressing is recommended except where soils are rich in potash

Nitrogen
✦ Is likely to be naturally present in reasonable quantities in good pasture or pastures containing clover
✦ Easily leached out by rain

Organic fertilizer
✦ This is farmyard manure, preferably from straw-bedded cattle that are not being fed with hormones and other nutrients that are toxic to horses.
✦ Contains phosphate which dissolves slowly into the soil, providing a steady supply
✦ Contains potash in a similar form to that found in inorganic fertilizer
✦ Contains nitrogen in a number of forms, some of which break down slowly for plant use
✦ Spread in autumn/winter or before a field is left to grow hay

Considering boundaries
● **Fences** are best positioned following contours rather than up and down them.
● **Fence off hazards** such as rabbit holes, oak trees (so horses don't eat acorns), stagnant pools.
● **Post and rail** is best (rails at 1.2m and 30–45cm/4ft and 12–18in from the ground). Posts should be on the outside of the fence, away from the horses and should end at the top rail.
● **Post and plain wire** with a top timber rail and taut wire is acceptable; the lowest strand 30–45cm (12–18in) from the ground.
● **Wire mesh** (sheep, pig or stock wire) needs to be used carefully to avoid horses getting their feet caught in it.
● **Hedges and banks** should be well maintained and without poisonous plants. They provide good shelter.
● **Electric fencing** is ideal for temporary enclosures – white tape or rope is most visible for horses and people. A single strand is usually adequate.
● Never use **barbed wire**. If barbed wire is already present, remove it or cordon it off with electric fencing.

Poisonous plants

These are key poisonous plants, but many others are also dangerous. Luckily, horses rarely eat poisonous plants unless there is nothing else to graze on. Therefore, ensure good grazing and supplemental feeding if necessary. Often these plants are more palatable when dry, so make sure they are not in your hay (see p.31).

✘ Black nightshade (*Solanum nigrum*)

✘ Bracken (*Pteridium*)

✘ Buttercup (*Ranunculus*)

✘ Foxglove (*Digitalis*)

✘ Horsetails (*Equisetum*)

✘ Laurel (*Laurus*)

✘ Deadly nightshade (*Atropa belladonna*)

✘ Privet (*Ligustrum*)

✘ Ragwort (*Senecio*) – the most common cause of livestock poisoning in the UK

✘ Rhododendron (*Rhododendron ponticum*)

✘ Yew (*Taxus*)

Worms and worming

✦ A typical lifecycle – eggs are passed out in dung, the larvae hatch and develop. After about a week they distribute themselves in water present on the surface of grass, the horse ingests them and they develop into the adult (egg-laying) worm in the horse's digestive system.

✦ Larvae are discouraged by dry pastures and low temperatures.

✦ Avoid grazing grass too low as most larvae are found close to the ground.

✦ Horses develop some resistance through exposure to low worm infestations, but no horse can cope with a large burden.

✦ Worm all horses in the yard at the same time with the same wormer.

✦ Worm new arrivals and keep them in for at least 48 hours before turning them out with other horses.

✦ Dose for worms 48 hours before moving horses to a clean pasture.

✦ For more worming guidelines, see 'A worming calendar', p.13.

A new pasture
Considerations for new pastures:

✦ Difficult and expensive – best done by contractors.

✦ Timing is weather dependent – spring and autumn are best.

✦ It needs about a year to settle before horses can be grazed on it.

✦ Choose a seed mix specially for horses, including plenty of late-flowering grasses.

✦ Incorporate some clover (not more than 30% coverage or the pasture becomes too rich).

✦ Consider some fescues for strength if horses are to be exercised in the field.

✦ Include some wild herbs if possible at the field margins.

A typical seed mix

Name	kg/ha	lb/acre
Perennial rye grass	18	16
Red fescue	5	4½
Crested dog's tail	1	1
Cocksfoot	2	2
Timothy	2	2
Meadow fescue	2	2
Clover	1	1
Total	**31**	**28½**

Herbs

Horses enjoy the following herbs in pasture and they are safely consumed in small quantities:

✔ Chicory (*Chicorium intybus*)

✔ Yarrow (*Achillea millefolium*)

✔ Great burnet (*Sanguisorba officinalis*)

✔ Dandelion (*Taraxacum officinale*)

✔ Ribwort plantain (*Plantago lanceolata*)

Pasture plants

Most grasses are more palatable when young, becoming less attractive later in the season or when not sufficiently grazed.

Name	Main qualities
Perennial rye grass (*Lolium perenne*)	Very palatable with good early and late growth
Italian rye grass (*Lolium multiflorum*)	Similar to perennial rye grass but less long lasting
Red fescue, Sheep's fescue (*Festuca rubra, F. ovina*)	Good turf, not highly nutritious
Meadow fescue (*Festuca pratensis*)	Good turf, very palatable, not highly nutritious
Crested dog's tail (*Cyanosurus cristatus*)	Hard wearing
Cocksfoot (*Dactylis glomerata*)	Hard wearing, early and late growth, very palatable
Yorkshire fog (*Holcus lanatus*)	Mid-season grower, not very palatable
Bents (*Agrostis* species)	Good turf, mid-season grower, not highly nutritious
Purple moorgrass, flying bent (*Molina caerulea*)	Grows rapidly, new growth is nutritious
Timothy (*Phleum pratense*)	Very palatable, valuable mid-season grass
Clover (*Trifolium repens, T. pratense*)	Improves soil fertility, drought resistant

From left to right:
White clover
Yorkshire fog
Bent

From left to right:
Sheep's fescue
Red fescue
Meadow fescue

From left to right:
Perennial rye grass
Timothy
Italian rye grass

Ideal stable

Yard design

Consider these features when choosing a livery yard (or designing your own yard). For grazing see p.38–41.

- Approval – is it approved by a recognized body such as the BHS? This means it will meet certain standards.
- Electricity – is there a safe supply and good lighting for dark mornings and evenings?
- Feed room – is it clean, dry and well-organized with a sink and kettle?
- Hay storage – is it separate from stables, dry and well-ventilated?
- Muck heap – is it away from the yard but easily accessed, and regularly cleared/restacked?
- Parking – is there a reasonable place in which to park while attending your horse?
- Safety – is the yard well kept and tidy without hazards that your horse could injure itself on?
- Security – are there good security systems in place? Consider both theft and fire.
- Stables – are they sheltered from prevailing weather? Wind and rain shouldn't blow into the stables.
- Storage – is there a covered area for tools and storage of rugs and bedding, and is it neat and tidy?
- Tack – is there a secure tack room or will you have to take your tack home?
- Turnout – is there plenty of good quality turnout? (See also pp.38–41.)
- Water – is the tap conveniently sited? Are there facilities for soaking hay?
- Yard – is it enclosed with a suitable dry, flat, easy to sweep surface?

Stable design

There should be:

- Adequate ventilation – roof vent or window (perspex or safety glass). The window should be on the same side as the door to prevent drafts but should not be blocked by the open top door.
- An overhang on the roof or a good gutter – to prevent rain dripping in.
- Solid flooring, preferably roughened concrete, inside and out.
- Floor slope for drainage.
- Safety bolts on the door, including a kick bolt at the bottom.
- Coach hooks to hold the doors open – doors should open outwards.
- Two tie rings – for the horse and the haynet.
- A well-protected light.
- Waterproof light switches well out of the horse's reach.
- Provision for water and feed buckets.

Bedding – a few pros and cons

Shavings – warm, dust-free, highly absorbent, easy to store, relatively cheap, may contain sharp pieces of wood or other rubbish, takes time to rot down.

Hemp – similar to shavings with the same qualities, but more expensive.

Straw – cheap, rots down well, may be eaten, less absorbent than other bedding, more wasteful as difficult to separate clean and dirty, not suitable for horses with respiratory problems.

Paper – warm, dust-free, rots down quickly, some horses are allergic to the ink, very absorbent but becomes heavy when damp, blows around in the yard, expensive.

Rubber matting – warm, dust-free, easy to clean, urine may collect underneath, heavy to lift when necessary.

Stable measurements

These are the ideal for a horse; ponies can manage in slightly smaller stables and may need a lower bottom door.

Stable – 4m (12ft) square

Doorway –1.1m (42in) wide

2.1m (7ft) high

2.7m (9ft) high

Bottom door – 1.2m (4ft) high

Perfect menage

The site

If you are lucky enough to have a choice of where to put your menage, consider the following points:

✦ Access – a surfaced track between stableyard and menage is essential in most cases, not only to prevent poaching from horse traffic but also to allow for maintenance.

✦ Distractions – seclusion from a busy road and other distractions will ensure better work from the horses.

✦ Drainage – build at ground level or above for best drainage.

✦ Electricity – for floodlighting and other uses.

✦ Fencing – the menage will need to be fenced and gated.

✦ Gradient – slopes will add to the cost of construction.

✦ Wind and weather – some shelter will be very much appreciated by all users.

Sizes

A standard menage is 20 x 40m (66 x 130ft), while one designed for international dressage competitions will be 20 x 60m (66 x 200ft). A width of 15m (50ft) is the minimum.

Simple schooling movements

A & B 6 to 20 metre circles and serpentines to improve horse's suppleness
C simple changes of rein across the long diagonals, centre line and halfway line will improve accuracy
D half circles back to the track to change the rein, improve horse suppleness and rider's dexterity

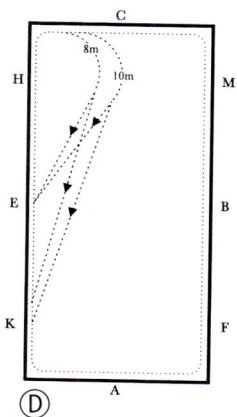

Construction

✦ Site levelled (levelled area at least 1m/3ft bigger than the menage on all sides) and drains and drainage pipes laid.

✦ Drainage membrane laid over the site.

✦ Foundation put down – the gravel drainage bed. The stones are around 50mm (2in) and the layer is 120mm (5in) or more.

✦ Next comes either a layer of smaller gravel for sand surfaces, to prevent the sand filtering into the drainage bed, or another membrane for other surfaces.

✦ Retaining boards are put in place around the perimeter – they should protrude 150mm (6in) above the school surface.

✦ The surface is laid.

Surfaces

Sand – cheap, safe and easily maintained. If it is allowed to become dirty (horse manure, fallen leaves), drainage can be a problem.

Woodchip – a strong, safe and cheap material that provides a good riding surface. It will need topping up annually as it decomposes and full replacement is required after about 6 years.

Granulated pvc – mixed with sand is high maintenance but long-lasting. It produces deeper going than sand and is ideal for young horses, giving a good springy surface.

Rubber (shreds or crumbs) – mixed with sand is excellent for jumping, long-lasting and low maintenance.

Gels – gel surfaces are very expensive but do provide a good surface, especially for jumping.

Feet and shoeing

No foot, no horse

Healthy well-cared for feet are vital to your horse's health and comfort as well as his ability to be able to do the work you ask of him.

Feet facts

● Front feet are round to increase their weight-carrying ability. They carry 60% of the horse's weight.

● Back feet are oval to aid propulsion – their main work.

● While the outer horn is non-living, the internal tissues of the feet are extremely sensitive.

● Hooves grow about 5mm (¼in) a month, more in summer less in winter. It takes about 6 months for a the horn to be replaced completely.

● The frog and sole also grow continuously.

● Diet has an influence on the quality of the horn and how fast it grows: grass rings (ridges on the hoof) indicate changes in the levels of nutrition.

● Calcium, zinc, methionine, biotin and sulphur all contribute to healthy horn growth but don't work if given in isolation.

● Most good quality food mixes contain enough nutrients, in the correct balance, to produce healthy horn.

● Shoeing protects the foot, but at the expense of some grip; an unshod horse is less likely to slip, especially on hard ground.

Foot care

✦ Pick out feet of stabled and grass-kept horses twice a day.

✦ Check for risen clenches or loose shoes every day.

✦ Check feet when you return from a ride to ensure nothing has caught in them.

✦ Keep horses out of very muddy pasture to avoid thrush, mud fever and other problems.

✦ Consider using hoof disinfectant to prevent foot problems.

✦ Maintain good stable hygiene to prevent thrush and other foot problems.

✦ For shod horses arrange for shoeing every 4–6 weeks, possibly more frequently in summer.

✦ For unshod horses arrange for trimming every 6–10 weeks, more frequently in summer.

Signs of a well-shod horse

✔ No light is visible between shoe and hoof.

✔ The horn is well trimmed but not dumped.

✔ The nails are placed towards the front of the hoof, to enable the heel to expand.

✔ The clenches are in a straight line along the hoof about one third of the way up.

✔ The clenches and clips are suitably seated.

✔ The heels are not too short, nor so long that they pressurize the frog.

✔ The horse is sound and moves freely.

✔ The shoe sits level on the ground without altering the way the horse stands.

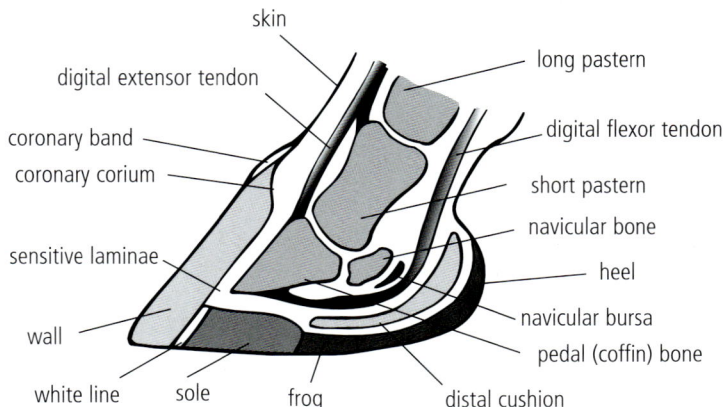

skin
long pastern
digital extensor tendon
coronary band
coronary corium
digital flexor tendon
short pastern
navicular bone
sensitive laminae
heel
navicular bursa
wall
pedal (coffin) bone
white line   sole   frog   distal cushion

Foot problems

Horses can suffer from a variety of foot problems, many of which may be diagnosed and/or treated by the farrier, including:

Abscess – see p.24.

Bruised sole – see p.28.

Corns – see p.28.

Sand cracks Vertical cracks in the hoof, sometimes caused by allowing feet to grow overlong. Shallow cracks can be treated by trimming and balancing the hoof; clips may be used to prevent them growing longer. Deep sand cracks can cause lameness and may have to be opened up and cut back to healthy horn along their length; the two sides of the crack may then be wired together or a bar shoe used.

Seedy toe Bacteria or fungi infect the white line, causing softening and crumbling, usually in the toe. Laminitis, infrequent trimming or stone damage may all be factors. The infected horn is cut back to healthy tissue, and remedial shoeing is often used.

Thrush – see p.24.

Some definitions

- **Bar shoe** – a shoe with closed heels for remedial shoeing, in cases of laminitis or fractured pedal bones, for example.
- **Cast** – a shoe that has come off.
- **Clench** – the bent over end of the nail in the hoof. Raised clenches stand proud of the hoof.
- **Clip** – a raised piece of metal drawn from the shoe to help keep it in position. There are usually two clips on a back shoe and one on a front shoe.
- **Dumped** – an over-rasped hoof.
- **Fullering** – the groove in the underside of the shoe, put there to improve grip and make the shoe lighter.
- **Nail** – used to fasten the shoe, the nail should sit comfortably in the nail hole. Traditionally, 3 nails are used on the inside and 4 on the outside, but the farrier will decide how many are necessary.
- **Nail bind or prick** – is when the newly inserted nail touches the sensitive part of the foot, causing lameness.
- **Plain stamped shoe** – a shoe without fullering, usually used for draught horses.
- **Remove** – a shoe that is reused, being replaced once the foot is trimmed.
- **Rolled toe shoe** – a shoe without clips and with the toe curved upwards to encourage a quick break over (the hoof leaving the ground) and reduce the risk of over-reaching.
- **Seat** – a small indentation made in the horn so that the clips and clenches fit flush with the rest of the hoof.

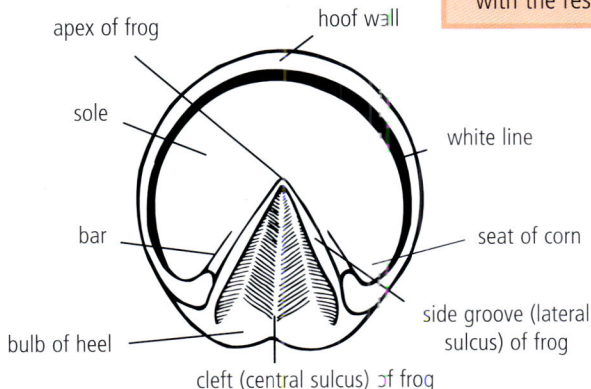

apex of frog

hoof wall

sole

white line

bar

seat of corn

bulb of heel

side groove (lateral sulcus) of frog

cleft (central sulcus) of frog

Saddles

Fit tips

Explain clearly what you want from your saddle when making the appointment with the saddler.

If your saddle is reflocked or adjusted in any way, your saddler must check it on your horse.

You and your horse can and should feel comfortable – if you don't like the saddle then it's no good.

Taking and using a wither pattern

✦ Use a flexicurve or flexible wire, such as a wire coat hanger.

✦ Place the flexicurve over the top of the withers.

✦ Shape it over the withers and around the shoulders. Smooth it all along its length, making sure you follow the contours exactly. Do one side then get someone to hold the curve in place while you move to the other (below left).

✦ Draw the resulting curve on a sheet of paper, noting nearside and offside – this is the wither pattern (below centre).

✦ Draw the curve onto cardboard and cut out the shape – this is the template.

✦ Get someone to hold up the saddle with the pommel towards you and fit the template into the saddle, lining it up with the points of the tree (below right).

✦ The saddle panels should fit snugly but not tightly around the template.

✦ There should be three fingers clearance into the pommel.

Fit checklist

● The front of the saddle sits 1cm (½in) behind the shoulder blade.

● The back of the saddle ends 15cm (6in) from the loin whorls.

● It touches the horse's back all along its length when girthed up.

● From the back of the saddle, slip your hand, palm downwards, under the panel. Beginning near the stirrup bar, run your hand backwards. There should be no restriction and the pressure should be even all along.

● The seat is horizontal to the ground.

● The cantle is slightly higher than the pommel.

● You can see through the length of the channel from front to back and its edges do not touch the backbone.

● The horse's shoulder is completely free to move naturally as he walks.

Signs of a poor fit

✗ Saddle slopes to front or slips forward in use – too wide.

✗ Saddle slopes to back – too narrow.

✗ Pinches, scuffed hair or uneven sweatmarks visible when the saddle is removed.

✗ The horse's performance is affected – reluctant go downhill, uneven shoe wear, takes a dislike to saddle.

A good saddle has:

✔ a wide weight-bearing surface – wide panels;

✔ smooth, soft, flat panels – run your fingers along their surface;

✔ a channel that is about 6cm (2½in) wide along its whole length;

✔ symmetry – above and below.

cantle

pommel

stud (nail)

seat

waist

skirt (covering stirrup bar)

gusseted panel

stirrup-leather keeper

saddle flap

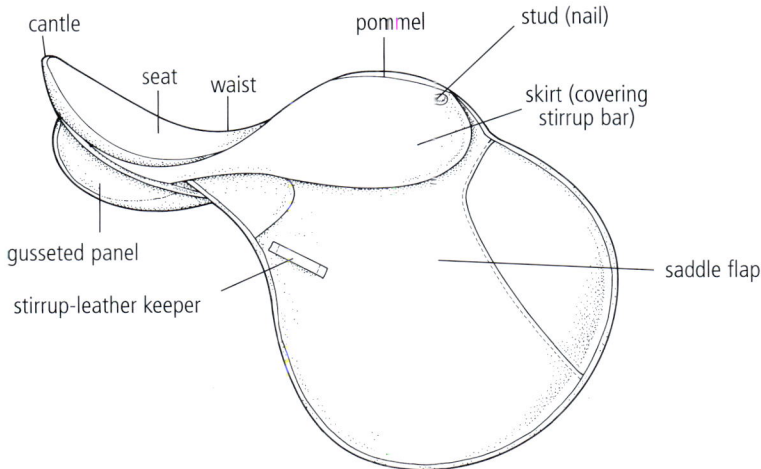

jumping saddle with forward-cut flaps

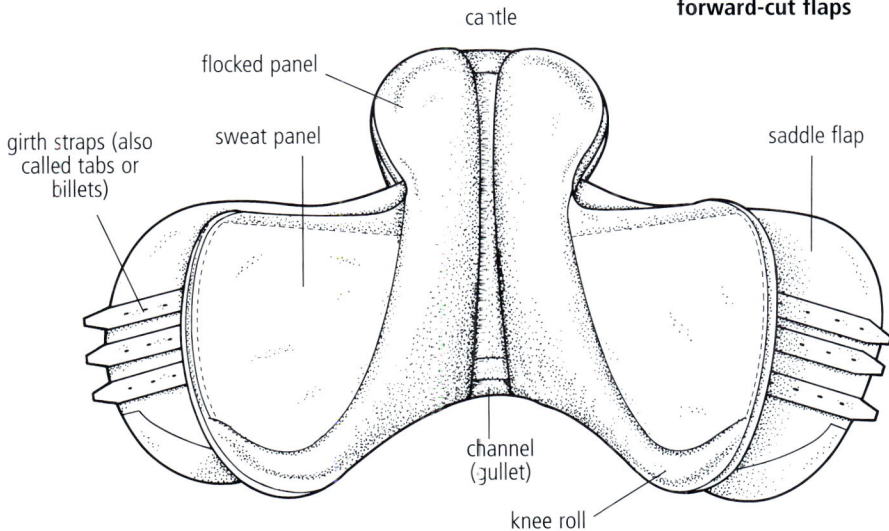

cantle

flocked panel

sweat panel

girth straps (also called tabs or billets)

saddle flap

channel (gullet)

knee roll

Saddle measurements
Width is the distance between the points of the tree.
Length is the measurement from the centre of the tree stud (nail) to the centre of the cantle.

Stirrup size
Ensure there is a 1cm (½in) gap between the riding boot and stirrup on each side.

Western saddles
Most of the fit checklist points (left) are relevant to fitting a Western saddle. Like an English saddle, a Western saddle should fit at the withers with clearance over the length of the backbone. It should not rub on the loins.

Bridles

Fitting a bridle

- Approximate sizes: pony to 14hh; cob 14–15hh; full 15–17hh.
- The browband fits around the brow without pulling at the back of the ears (too short) or slipping or flapping at the front (too long).
- The throatlash is done up loosely so that you can fit your hand's width between the horse's cheek and the throatlash (below left).
- A cavesson noseband sits one to two finger's width below the cheekbone and two fingers can slip between it and the horse's face (below right).
- A drop noseband sits 7cm (3in) above the horse's nostrils and one finger can slip between it and the horse's muzzle. It is vital not to have it too low as it will restrict the horse's breathing.
- Flash nosebands fit in the same way as a cavesson, with the flash strap buckled at the back of the jaw and tight enough to allow one finger to slip between it and the horse's muzzle.
- The bit should be high enough in the mouth to give the horse a slight smile, not a grimace. Check its width by straightening it gently in the horse's mouth – you should be able to fit your little finger between the bit cheekpiece and the horse's lips on both sides.

Bit size

Straighten the bit and measure from the inside of one cheekpiece to the inside of the other.

Fitting a curb chain

The chain sits gently in the chin groove at the back of the jaw and comes into action when the curb cheeks are drawn back by 45 degrees.

- Attach the end link to the offside curb hook.
- Holding the chain at both ends, twist it clockwise until the links lie flat and the flylink hangs down.
- Hook the last link to the nearside curb hook.
- Check fit by pulling back gently on the reins.
- Unhook and use the next link in if necessary, keeping the links flat.

Martingales

- Martingale neck straps should fit near the withers and be loose enough to allow a hand's width between strap and wither.
- Standing martingale – with the horse's head in the correct position, lift the martingale up towards the neck. It should just reach the throat.
- Running martingale – with the martingale attached at the girth, bring both rings to one side of the horse's neck; they should reach the withers.

Tack cleaning tips

- ✔ Use a damp cloth to wipe off mud.
- ✔ Use washing up liquid and water sparingly on very greasy areas; rinse well and allow to dry.
- ✔ Use saddle soap to feed, as well as clean.
- ✔ Use a clean dry cloth to produce a shine.
- ✔ Periodically, use leather dressing, but not on flocked panels as it spoils 'loft'.

snaffle bridle

- headpiece
- browband
- throatlash (throatlatch)
- noseband
- keepers
- cheekpieces
- hooked billet
- reins
- eggbutt snaffle

Double bridle

A double bridle has:

- two bits: a bridoon (a light snaffle) and a curb;
- a second headpiece (a sliphead) with one cheekpiece (on off side). This fits under the headpiece and secures the bridoon, while the curb bit is secured on the bridle cheekpieces;
- a lip strap to hold the curb chain should it become detached and to prevent the horse grabbing the cheeks of the curb bit;
- two sets of reins, one for each bit.

Fit a double bridle in the same way as a snaffle bridle (see left) but:

- make the throatlash marginally looser;
- lower the noseband very slightly;
- fit the bridoon above the curb – slightly higher in the mouth than a single bit would be.

double bridle

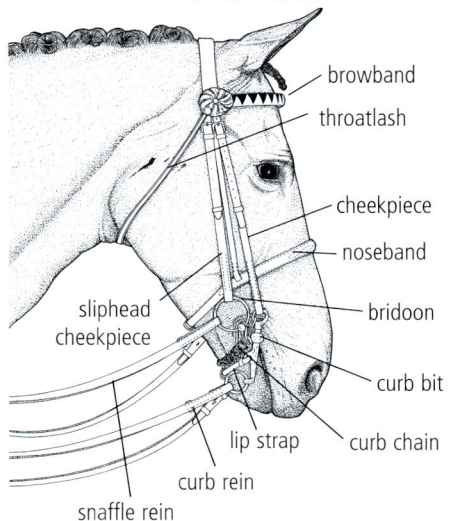

- browband
- throatlash
- cheekpiece
- noseband
- bridoon
- sliphead cheekpiece
- curb bit
- lip strap
- curb chain
- curb rein
- snaffle rein

A guide to riding terms

Canter (**lope**) is a pace with three beats and a moment of suspension: in canter the beats are even – 1,2,3 1,2,3 – in lope they are uneven – 1, 2-3, 1, 2-3. Right lead is left hind, left fore and right hind together, right fore, suspension. Left lead is right hind, right fore and left hind together, left fore, suspension. Canter on a right lead when riding clockwise, a left lead when riding anti-clockwise. Counter canter is when these leads are reversed in advanced work; false canter is when this happens unintentionally. The lead can be seen by the rider as a more pronounced forward and backward movement of the leading shoulder: in left lead this is seen in the left shoulder.

Collection is seen in trot and canter, and variation on these paces, such as piaffe and passage. The horse's strides are shortened until they become very light and springy. The horse feels very agile and manoeuvrable.

Contact is the link between the horse's mouth and the rider's hands through the reins. A horse must accept contact before he can learn to be on the bit, while the rider must learn to ride in balance, without leaning on the reins, and develop 'soft' giving hands.

Diagonals Trot on the right diagonal when going anti-clockwise (to the left) and on the left diagonal when going clockwise (to the right). Trotting on the right diagonal involves sitting when the horse's right fore and left hind touch the ground and rising as they leave the ground – this can be seen by the rider as the horse's right shoulder moving backward (foot touching the ground) then forward (leaving the ground). Rise as the outside shoulder moves forward and sit as it moves back.

Extended paces are where the horse covers the most ground at walk, trot and canter by taking longer strides at greater speed than the medium or working paces while maintaining the same rhythm.

Flying change is where the canter lead is changed from right to left, or vice versa, without altering the pace or rhythm. The change is requested by altering the leg aids during the moment of suspension.

Gallop, the fastest pace, has four rapid beats. Right lead gallop is left hind, right hind, left fore, right fore, suspension. Left lead is right hind, left hind, right fore, left fore, suspension.

Half pass is where the horse, bent around the rider's inside leg and in the direction of travel, moves sideways and forwards on the diagonal making two tracks. The forehand is slightly ahead of the quarters. The outside legs cross in front of the inside legs so if the direction of movement is left to right the left legs cross in front of the right legs. Half pass is performed in collected trot or collected canter.

Impulsion is created by the rider's legs, so that the horse feels as if it has boundless, contained energy coming from the quarters.

In front of the leg is when the horse accepts and reponds instantly to the lightest leg aids, without rushing and remaining in balance.

Inside leg and/or hand is nearest the centre of the school. On a circle or turn the horse bends around the inside leg.

Jog is a Western trot in slow-time with less knee action than in a dressage-type trot.

Leg yield The horse moves both sideways and forwards with the inside legs crossing in front of the outside legs; there is a slight bend at the poll. Performed in either walk or working trot.

Medium paces are between working and extended. While the speed and rhythm remain the same as in the working pace, the stride lengthens so increasing the ground covered. In medium walk the horse should overtrack.

On the bit A horse is on the bit when his energy is coming through from his hindquarters to the forehand, which is light. He accepts the bit softly, his neck arched and raised but supple, and he is in self-carriage, making a rounded, powerful and elegant outline.

Outside leg and/or hand is the one nearest the outer edge of the school. On a circle or turn the outside leg acts behind the girth to encourage the quarters in the turn.

Passage is a rhythmic, collected and springy trot; each diagonal pair of feet is lifted very high and the moment of suspension is prolonged.

Piaffe is a springy trot performed on the spot, rhythmically and with great collection.

Rein back is almost two-time (like trot) with diagonal pairs of legs moving back together.

Renvers/travers (haunches out, haunches in) The horse moves forwards and sideways with the quarters out (renvers) or in (travers), bending around the rider's leg and making four tracks. The difference between the two is only in the horse's original position: in renvers his forehand leaves the track, in travers his quarters leave the track.

Self-carriage is where a horse carries himself lightly and in balance with more of his weight on his haunches so that he is able to take the additional weight of a rider and perform school movements without falling onto his forehand.

Shoulder in is where the horse bends around the rider's inside leg, bringing the forehand off the straight line so making three tracks with the inside fore crossing in front of the outside fore. The trot must be at least slightly collected.

Tracking up is when the horse's hind feet step into the tracks made by his forefeet in walk. Overtracking, where the hind feet over step the tracks by anything up to 30cm (12in), is an indicator of a good, long-striding, free walk. An under tracking horse is likely to be young or unschooled, while hind foot prints to one side of the forefoot prints may indicate stiffness.

Trot is a pace with two even beats. Diagonal pairs of feet touch the ground together: the sequence is right fore and left hind, suspension, left fore and right hind, suspension.

Turn on the forehand is when the horse's hindquarters turn around the forehand at walk. If the quarters move right, the left hindleg crosses in front of the right hindleg; if they move left, the right hindleg crosses in front of the left hindleg. The forelegs step on the spot while the hindlegs describe part of a circle.

Turn on the haunches or pirouette is when the horse's forehand turns around the quarters at walk or canter. The inside hind foot is the pivot around which the forelegs and outside hind foot move. The outside foreleg crosses in front of the inside foreleg, while the outside hind moves around the inside hind which returns to more or less the same spot each time it is lifted.

Walk is a pace with four even beats, like a march: a sequence is left hind, left fore, right hind, right fore. There are always at least two feet on the ground.

Working paces are trot and canter performed at a steady rhythm, balance and speed. They are used for schooling horses as yet untrained in medium, extended and collected paces.

A brief guide to jumps

An **arrowhead** looks like a triangle when viewed from above. The horse has to jump into it via the point, and then jump out.
A **bounce** is two or more jumps in a row positioned closely with no non-jumping strides in between, so the horse lands and immediately takes off again.
A **coffin** is a combination of jumps involving a rail to jump in, a ditch on lower ground and a rail to jump out.
A **corner** forms a V-shape. Both arms of the V are cleared together near its point.
A **drop** is any jump that involves landing on ground lower than that you took off from.
A **Normandy bank** is a combination of a jump up onto a flat bank and a jump out over a rail with a drop on the far side.
An **oxer** is a wide jump with rails, a hedge and possibly a ditch.
A **parallel** is two sets of rails at the same height (unlike a staircase).
A **pyramid** is any jump where the middle section is highest, as in a tiger trap.
A **spread** is a wide jump.
A **staircase** is a jump consisting of two or more bars with the back bar(s) higher than the front one(s).
A **tiger trap** is formed with two sets of rails sloping so that they lean against each other, making an upside down V-shape when viewed from the side.
A **trakehner** is an upright with a ditch under it.
An **upright** is a simple single jump.

January

When God had created the horse,
He spoke to the magnificent creature:
'I have made thee unlike any other.
All the treasures of this earth lie between thine eyes…
Thou shall fly without wings
And conquer without sword.'

The Koran

January 2004

Monday	29
Tuesday	30
Wednesday	31
Thursday	1 New Year's Day, Bank Holiday UK & Rep of Ireland
Friday	2 Bank Holiday Scotland
Saturday	3
Sunday	4

● Decide on your aims and ambitions for the year
● Look out for rug rubs, adjusting fit if necessary

January 2004

5

6   Epiphany

7

8

9

10

11

Look out for frozen water troughs

Monday 12

Tuesday 13

Wednesday 14

Thursday 15

Friday 16

Saturday 17

Sunday 18

●Monitor your horse's weight (p.34), increasing hay and feed if necessary

January 2004

Monday 19 Martin Luther King Jr Day USA

Tuesday 20

Wednesday 21

Thursday 22 Chinese New Year

Friday 23

Saturday 24

Sunday 25

●Watch for mud fever (p.29), rainscald (p.30), thrush (p.24)

January/February 2004

Monday	26	
Tuesday	27	Australia Day
Wednesday	28	Desert Circuit begins (ends 7 March)
Thursday	29	
Friday	30	
Saturday	31	
Sunday	1	

On freezing mornings give extra hay to grass-kept horses

February

The one great precept and practice in using a horse is this — never deal with him when you are in a fit of passion. A fit of passion is a thing that has no foresight in it, and so we often have to rue the day when we gave way to it.

Xenophon

February 2004

Monday 2

Tuesday 3

Wednesday 4

Thursday 5

Friday 6
Waitangi Day NZ

Saturday 7

Sunday 8

● Watch for mud fever (p.29), rainscald (p.30), thrush (p.24)
● Watch for rug rubs, adjusting fit if necessary

February 2004

9

10

11

12

13

14   St Valentine's Day

15

- Look out for frozen water troughs
- Book the equine dentist (p.20)

February 2004

Monday 16

Tuesday 17

Wednesday 18

Thursday 19

Friday 20

Saturday 21

Sunday 22

- Check your horse's vaccinations are up-to-date (p.12)
- Administer late winter wormer, if necessary (p.13)

February 2004

Monday 23

Tuesday 24 Shrove Tuesday

Wednesday 25

Thursday 26

Friday 27

Saturday 28

Sunday 29

● Monitor your horse's weight (p.34), increasing hay and feed if necessary
● On freezing mornings give extra hay to grass-kept horses

March

... I like to ride
When all the world is in bed,
To the top of the hill where the sky grows wide,
And where the sun grows red.

Wilfred Scawen Blunt *The Old Squire*

March 2004

Monday 1   St David's Day

Tuesday 2

Wednesday 3

Thursday 4

Friday 5

Saturday 6

Sunday 7   Desert Circuit ends (begins 28 January)

● Harrow and roll pastures (p.38)

March 2004

Monday 8

Tuesday 9

Wednesday 10

Thursday 11

Friday 12

Saturday 13

Sunday 14

● Change to a lighter rug on warm dry days

March 2004

15

16

17
St Patrick's Day, Bank Holiday Rep of Ireland

18

19

20

21
Mothering Sunday

●Check for emerging ragwort and other poisonous plants (p.31)

March 2004

Monday
22

Tuesday
23

Wednesday
24
Ash Wednesday

Thursday
25

Friday
26

Saturday
27

Sunday
28
Grand Prix of Tampa, British Summer Time begins

● Start spring worming programme (p.13)

March/April 2004

Monday 29

Tuesday 30

Wednesday 31

Thursday 1
All Fool's Day

Friday 2

Saturday 3
Budweiser American Invitational Grand Prix

Sunday 4
Palm Sunday

April

Horses are often gruff and rough among themselves but they never show rage or rancour; these are typically human qualities that have no place in the interaction with a horse.

Klaus Ferdinand Hempfling *Dancing with Horses*

April 2004

Monday **5**

Tuesday **6**   First Day of Passover

Wednesday **7**

Thursday **8**

Friday **9**   Good Friday Holiday UK & Rep of Ireland

Saturday **10**

Sunday **11**   Easter Day

● Harrow and roll pastures (p.38)

April 2004

Monday 12

Tuesday 13

Wednesday 14

Thursday 15

Friday 16   Party   Dan Carrs

Saturday 17

Sunday 18

- Beware of grazing conditions that are likely to induce laminitis (p.25)
- Continue worming as necessary (p.13)

April 2004

Monday	**19**	Off 1day owed good friday
Tuesday	**20**	Off
Wednesday	**21**	off — Birthday of Queen Elizabeth II
Thursday	**22**	
Friday	**23**	St George's Day
Saturday	**24**	
Sunday	**25**	

● Change to a lighter rug on warm dry days, leave rugs off in really nice weather
● Check for ragwort and other poisonous plants (p.31)

April/May 2004

ANZAC Day AUS/NZ

Monday 26

Tuesday 27

Wednesday 28

Thursday 29 west life

Friday 30

Saturday 1

Sunday 2

● Brush your horse regularly to remove loose hair

May

As May was opening the rosebuds,
elder and lilac beginning to bloom,
it was time for the mare to foal.

Ferenc Juhász *Birth of the Foal*

May 2004

Monday | 3 — Mums B'day — Early May Bank Holiday UK & Rep of Ireland

Tuesday | 4

Wednesday | 5

Thursday | 6 — Badminton Horse Trials begins

Friday | 7

Saturday | 8

Sunday | 9 — Badminton Horse Trials ends

Remove rugs, repair and clean them

May 2004

10

11

12

13

14

15

16

● Monitor your horse's weight (p.34), reduce grazing and feed if necessary

Monday 17

Tuesday 18

Wednesday 19

Thursday 20   Ascension Day – Holy Thursday

Friday 21

Saturday 22

Sunday 23

● Check for ragwort and other poisonous plants (p.31)

May 2004

Monday 24

Tuesday 25

Wednesday 26 — Feast of Weeks (Shavuot)

Thursday 27

Friday 28

Saturday 29

Sunday 30 — Whit Sunday

May/June 2004

Monday | 31 | Spring Bank Holiday UK, Memorial Day USA

Tuesday | 1 | Coronation Day

Wednesday | 2 |

Thursday | 3 |

Friday | 4 |

Saturday | 5 |

Sunday | 6 | Trinity Sunday

● Remove rugs, repair and clean them

June

The hoofs of the horses! Oh! witching and sweet
Is the music earth steals from the iron-shod feet;
No whisper of lover, no trilling of bird,
Can stir me as hoofs of the horses have stirred.

Will H. Ogilvie *Galloping Shoes*

June 2004

Monday 7

Bank Holiday Rep of Ireland

Tuesday 8

Wednesday 9

Thursday 10

Corpus Christi, Birthday of Prince Philip Duke of Edinburgh

Friday 11

Saturday 12

Sunday 13

● Check water troughs for cleanliness, removing algae and dead vegetation

June 2004

Monday 14 — The Queen's official birthday, Flag Day USA

Tuesday 15

Wednesday 16

Thursday 17

Friday 18

Saturday 19

Sunday 20 — Father's Day, Paint Horse World Show begins

Monitor your horse's weight (p.34), reduce grazing and feed if necessary

Monday 21

Tuesday 22

Wednesday 23

Thursday 24

Friday 25

Saturday 26

Sunday 27

Give your horse a bath on a warm dry still day

June/July 2004

Monday 28

Tuesday 29

Wednesday 30

Thursday 1
Canada Day

Friday 2

Saturday 3
Paint Horse World Show ends

Sunday 4
Independence Day USA

● Check water troughs for cleanliness, removing algae and dead vegetation

July

'You can keep your buses and cars,
I'll take a horse.'
'A horse?'
'Yes.'
Don't be mad;
What would you do with a horse?'
'Ride it, of course...'

Sid Delaney *A Horse in the City*

July 2004

Monday	**5**
Tuesday	**6**
Wednesday	**7** Tevis Cup (Western States Trail Ride) begins
Thursday	**8**
Friday	**9**
Saturday	**10**
Sunday	**11**

● Get ready for hay/haylage making

July 2004

Monday 12

Tuesday 13

Wednesday 14

Thursday 15

Friday 16

Saturday 17

Sunday 18

● Book the equine dentist

July 2004

Monday | 19

Tuesday | 20

Wednesday | 21

Thursday | 22

Friday | 23

Saturday | 24

Sunday | 25

Give your horse a bath on a warm dry still day

July/August 2004

Monday 26

Tuesday 27

Wednesday 28

Thursday 29

Friday 30

Saturday 31

Sunday 1

August

Riding is a partnership. The horse lends you his strength, speed and grace, which are greater than yours… you give him your guidance, intelligence and understanding, which are greater than his.

Lucy Rees *Riding: The True Techniques*

August 2004

Monday 2

Tuesday 3

Wednesday 4

Thursday 5

Friday 6

Saturday 7

Sunday 8

Check water troughs for cleanliness, removing algae and dead vegetation

August 2004

Monday 9

Tuesday 10

Wednesday 11

Thursday 12

Friday 13 — Olympic Games begin

Saturday 14

Sunday 15

● Buy new rugs

August 2004

Monday 16

Tuesday 17

Wednesday 18

Thursday 19

Friday 20

Saturday 21

Sunday 22

● Clean and repair rugs

August 2004

Monday 23

Tuesday 24

Wednesday 25

Thursday 26

Friday 27

Saturday 28

Sunday 29   Olympic Games end

• Watch out for bot fly eggs

August/September 2004

Monday
30
Bank Holiday England, Wales & Northern Ireland

Tuesday
31

Wednesday
1

Thursday
2
Burghley Horse Trials begins

Friday
3

Saturday
4

Sunday
5
Burghley Horse Trials ends

● Rugs on

September

*Dappled and silver-white,
With a mane
Like drifting smoke…*

Llywelyn Lucas *The Dustman's Horse*

September 2004

6 Monday
Labor Day USA/CAN

7 Tuesday

8 Wednesday

9 Thursday

10 Friday

11 Saturday

12 Sunday
Grandparents' Day USA

Plan your clipping calendar

September 2004

13

14

15

16

Jewish New Year 5765 (Rosh Hashanah)

17

18

19

Beware of grazing conditions that are likely to induce laminitis (p.25)

September 2004

Monday 20

Tuesday 21

Wednesday 22
Paralympic Games begin

Thursday 23

Friday 24

Saturday 25
Day of Atonement (Yom Kippur)

Sunday 26

Watch out for bot fly eggs

September/October 2004

Monday 27
Paralympic Games end

Tuesday 28

Wednesday 29

Thursday 30
First Day of Tabernacles (Succoth)

Friday 1

Saturday 2

Sunday 3

● Administer wormer, particularly for tapeworm (or October) (p.13)

October

As I rode home through woods that smelled of evening,
my horse reined up on his intuitive will
and stood, ears cocked, hearing his visible breathing,
the only sound alive this side the hill.

Maurice Lindsay, *The Fall of the Leaf*

October 2004

Monday	4
Tuesday	5
Wednesday	6 Horse of the Year Show begins
Thursday	7
Friday	8
Saturday	9
Sunday	10 Horse of the Year Show ends

● Rugs on
● Wear high visibility kit when riding

October 2004

Monday
11
Columbus Day USA/Thanksgiving Day CAN

Tuesday
12

Wednesday
13

Thursday
14
First Day of Ramadan

Friday
15

Saturday
16

Sunday
17

- Check water troughs for leaves
- Clip if necessary

October 2004

Monday 18

Monday 18

Tuesday 19

Wednesday 20

Thursday 21

Friday 22

Saturday 23

Sunday 24

● Beware of grazing conditions that are likely to induce laminitis (p.25)
● Increase feed and give hay (p.34)

October 2004

Monday | 25 | Public Holiday Rep of Ireland

Tuesday | 26

Wednesday | 27

Thursday | 28

Friday | 29

Saturday | 30

Sunday | 31 | British Summer Time ends, Hallowe'en

●Administer wormer, particularly for tapeworm (p.13)

November

Hacking home in the moonlight, slowly,
You and I on the silver road,
Tired and stiff, but contented wholly
With the blessings the day bestowed.

Edric Roberts *Blessings*

November 2004

Monday 1

Tuesday 2

Wednesday 3

Thursday 4

Friday 5

Saturday 6   Equine Event

Sunday 7   Equine Event

● Keep a check for mud fever (p.29), rainscald (p.30) thrush (p.24)

November 2004

Monday | 8

Tuesday | 9

Wednesday | 10

Thursday | 11   Veterans' Day USA

Friday | 12

Saturday | 13

Sunday | 14   Remembrance Sunday

● Look out for frozen water troughs

November 2004

15

16

17

18

19

20

21

●Laminitis can still occur in suspectible horses (p.25)

November 2004

Monday 22

Tuesday 23

Wednesday 24

Thursday 25   Thanksgiving Day USA

Friday 26

Saturday 27

Sunday 28

Administer wormer, particularly for bots (or December) (p.13)

November/December 2004

Monday	29
Tuesday	30 · St Andrew's Day
Wednesday	1
Thursday	2
Friday	3
Saturday	4
Sunday	5

● Monitor your horse's weight (p.34), increasing hay and feed if necessary
● On freezing mornings give extra hay to grass-kept horses

December

If one induces the horse
To assume that carriage
Which it would adopt
Of its own accord when displaying its beauty,
Then, one directs the horse
To appear joyous and magnificent,
Proud and remarkable
For having been ridden.

Xenophon

December 2004

Monday 6

Tuesday 7

Wednesday 8

Thursday 9

Friday 10

Saturday 11

Sunday 12

● Keep a check for mud fever (p.29), rainscald (p.30), thrush (p.24)
● Look out for frozen water troughs

December 2004

Monday 13

Tuesday 14

Wednesday 15

Thursday 16   Olympia begins

Friday 17

Saturday 18

Sunday 19

●Watch out for rug rubs, adjusting fit if necessary

December 2004

Monday 20   Olympia ends

Tuesday 21

Wednesday 22

Thursday 23

Friday 24

Saturday 25   Christmas Day

Sunday 26   Boxing Day, St Stephen's Day

● Administer wormer, particularly for bots (p.13)

December/January 2004/5

27

28

Wednesday

29

Thursday

30

Friday

31

Saturday

1   New Year's Eve

Sunday

2   New Year's Day

● Monitor your horse's weight (p.34), increasing hay and feed if necessary

January 2005

3

4

5

6

7

8

9

On freezing mornings give extra hay to grass-kept horses

Notes

Useful Addresses

Equine associations, shows and fairs UK

British Dressage National Agricultural Centre, Stoneleigh Park, Warwickshire CV8 2LR. Tel. 024 76698830; Fax. 024 76790390. www.britishdressage.co.uk

British Eventing, National Agricultural Centre, Stoneleigh Park, Warwickshire CV8 2LR. Tel. 024 7669 8856; Fax. 024 7669 7235. www.britisheventing.co.uk

British Equestrian Trade Association,, East Wing, Stockeld Park, Wetherby, West Yorkshire LS22 4AW. www.beta-uk.org

British Horse Society, Stoneleigh Deer Park, Kenilworth, Warwickshire CV8 2XZ. Tel. 08701 202 244; Fax. 01926 707 800. www.bhs.org.uk
The BHS is the largest equine charity in Britain. It is dedicated to improving the welfare of horses and ponies through education and can supply information on a wide range of equestrian subjects.

British Show Jumping Association, National Agricultural Centre, Stoneleigh Park, Warwickshire CV8 2LR. Tel. 024 7669 8800; Fax. 024 7669 6685. www.bsja.co.uk

Contour Exhibitions and Events Limited, Suite 7, Swallow Court, Devonshire Gate, Tiverton, Devon EX16 7EJ. Tel. 01884 841644; Fax. 01884 841647. www.contour.uk.net
Details of the four equine fairs held in Britain each year: South West, North of England, Scottish, Midlands.

Veteran Horse Society, Hendre Fawr Farm, St Dogmaels, Cardigan, SA43 3LZ. Fax. 01239 881310. www.veteran-horse-society.co.uk

Equine businesses and general websites

www.adas.co.uk Head office ADAS Wolverhampton HQ, Woodthorne, Wergs Road, Wolverhampton WV6 8TQ. Consultancies and research centres throughout England and Wales. Tel. 0845 766 0085. The ADAS (Agricultural Development Advisory Service) can help with soil and feed analysis and other equine management issues.
www.athens.olympic.org The official website for the Athens Olympic Games.
www.horseandhound.co.uk Details of all sorts of horsey events, etc.
www.horseit.com Useful website with plenty of information on horse care and links to other horsey sites.
www.horsetrace.com Horsetrace Ltd, Armyn Cross, Minety, Wiltshire SN16 9RJ. This organization offers ways for you to find information about your horse and helps to trace stolen horses.

Equine associations, shows and fairs US

Kentucky Horse Park, 4089 Iron Works, Parkway, Lexington, Kentucky KY 40511-8462. Tel. 859 233 4303 (TDD), 800 678 8813 (toll free); Fax. 859 254 0253. www.imh.org/khp The horse park is a working horse farm and museum dedicated to the relationship between man and the horse. The website has links to a vast number of equestrian organizations, clubs, magazines, etc.

National Future Farmers of America (FFA) Center, P.O. Box 68960, 6060 FFA Drive, Indianapolis, IN 46268-0960. Tel. 317 802 6060; Fax. 317 802 6061. www.ffa.org. The FFA has details of the Horse Proficiency Program and other information.

The American Horse Council, 1616 H Street NW, 7th Floor, Washington, DC 20006. Tel. 202 296 4031; Fax. 202 296 1970. www.horsecouncil.org/ahc.html The American Horse Council can sell you a Horse Industry Directory, which lists breed and performance associations.

United States Equestrian Team, Pottersville Road, P.O. Box 355, Gladstone, New Jersey, NJ 07934. Tel. 908 234 1251; Fax. 908 234 9417. www.uset.com A non-profit-making organization providing training, equipment and finance to skilled equestrians to enable them to enter major international competitions.

United States Pony Clubs, Inc, 4041 Iron Works Parkway, Lexington, Kentucky KY 40511-8462. Tel. 859 254 7669; Fax. 859 233 4652. www.ponyclub.org

4-H National 4-H Headquarters, 1400 Independence Avenue SW, Washington DC 20250-2225 www.national4-hheadquarters.gov

Equine health

Equilibrium Products Ltd, Unit 7 Upper Wingbury Farm, Leighton Road, Wingrave, Buckinghamshire HP22 4LW. Tel. 01296 682681; Fax. 01296 680345. www.equilibriumproducts.com
Manufacturers of muzzle nets for headshakers.

Equine Grass Sickness Fund, Moredun foundation, Pentlands Science Park, Penicuik, Midlothian EH26 0PZ. Tel. 0131 445 6257; Fax. 0131 445 6235. www.grasssickness.org.uk
Research into grass sickness and information and support for owners of horses that contract the disease.

Horses & Courses Ltd., Crawley Grange, North Crawley, Buckinghamshire MK16 9HL. Tel. 01727 751133; Fax. 08707 065295. www.horsesandcourses.co.uk
Correspondence college offering short courses in horse-related subjects.

Palm's Rest,
Arlington Close, Undy, Monmouthshire NP26 3EF. Tel.
0871 717 9808; Fax. 0871 717 9809. www.equine-
farewells.com A service offering equine
funerals.

The Laminitis Trust.
Helpline Tel. 0905 105 105 1. www.laminitis.org
Information about laminitis prevention, treatment, drug
trials and much more.

www.pcweb.liv.ac.uk/sarcoids/index.ssi A website
devoted to providing information on sarcoids and their
treatment. Linked to the Division of Equine Studies,
University of Liverpool.

Equine charities UK

Ada Cole Rescue Stables, Broadlands, Broadley
Common, Near Nazeing, Waltham Abbey, Essex EN9 2DH.
Tel. 01992 892133; Fax. 01992 893841.
www.adacole.co.uk

Blue Cross Head Office, Shilton Road, Burford,
Oxfordshire OX18 4PF. Tel. 01993 825500; Fax. 01993
823083. www.bluecross.org.uk

Brooke Hospital for Animals, Broadmead House, 21
Panton Street, London SW1Y 4DR. Tel. 020 7930 0210;
Fax. 020 7930 2386. www.brookehospital.com

Heavy Horse Rest & Rescue, Plas y Gwynt,
Llanfaethlu, Isle of Anglesey LL65 4PA. Tel. 01407
730757. www.heavyhorserestandrescue.com

Home of Rest for Horses, Westcroft Stables, Speen
Farm, Slad Lane, Princes Risborough, Buckinghamshire
HP27 0PP. Tel.01494 488 464; Fax. 01494 488 767.
www.hcmeofrestforhorses.co.uk

Horses and Ponies Protection Association, The
Stables, Burnley Wharf, Manchester Road, Burnley,
Lancashire BB11 1JZ. Tel. 01282 455992; Fax. 01282
451992. www.happa.org.uk

International League for the Protection of Horses,
Anne Colvin House, Snetterton, Norfolk NR16 2LR. Tel.
0870 870 1927; Fax. 0870 904 1927. www.ilph.org
Cruelty Hotline: Tel. 0870 871 1927.

Redwings Horse Sanctuary, Hapton, Norwich NR15
1SP. Tel. 01508 481000; Fax. 0870 458 1947. Welfare
Hotline: Tel. 01508 481008. www.redwings.co.uk

The Donkey Sanctuary, Slade House Farm, Salcombe
Regis, Sidmouth, Devon EX10 0NU.

Riding charities US

www.cyberodeo.com
www.horses.about.com/cs/therapeuticriding These sites
provide information on a number of organizations
offering therapeutic riding for disabled riders or those
requiring special facilities.

Equine charities US

American Horse Defense Fund,
11206 Valley View Drive, Kensington MD 20895.
Tel. 1 866 983 3456 (toll free). www.ahdf.org/

California Equine Retirement Foundation,
34033 Kooden Road, Winchester, CA 92596.
Tel. 909 926 4190; Fax. 909 926 4181.
www.cerfhorses.org

Equine Rescue League,
Inc., PO Box 4366, Leesburg, Virginia 20177.
Tel. 703 771 1240. www.equineresueleague.org

Hooved Animal Humane Society,
P.O. Box, 400, 10804 McConnell Road, Woodstock,
IL 60098. Tel. 815 337 5563; Fax. 815 337 5569.
www.hahs.org

Horse Rescue and Relief Retirement Fund,
1768 Newt Green Road, Cumming, Georgia 30040.
Tel. 770 886 5419. www.savethehorses.org

Thoroughbred Retirement Foundation,
450 Shrewsbury Plaza, Shrewsbury, MJ 07702-4332.
Tel. 732 957 0182. www.trfinc.org

Riding charities UK

Fortune Centre of Riding Therapy,
Avon Tyrell, Bransgore, Christchurch, Dorset BH23 8EE.
Tel. 01425 673297; Fax. 01425 674320. www.fortune-
centre.org An organization to use horses and riding to
help young people with behavioural problems.

Mark Davies Injured Riders Fund,
38 Regent on the River, William Morris Way, London SW6
2UT. Tel./Fax. 0207 736 1738. www.mdirf.co.uk

Riding For the Disabled Association,
Lavinia Norfolk House, Avenue R, Stoneleigh Park,
Warwickshire CV8 2LY. Tel. 024 7669 6510;
Fax. 024 7669 6532.
www.riding-for-disabled.org.uk

Equine associations, AUS and NZ

The Australian Pony Club Council Inc.
National Secretariat: P.O. Box 206
TWEED HEADS 2485
www.ponyclub-australia.org

Australian Veterinary Association
PO Box 371, Artarmon, NSW 1570, Australia
www.ava.com.au

New Zealand Veterinary Association
PO Box 11-212, Manners Street, Wellington, New Zealand
www.vets.org.nz